THE SELF PARENTING PROGRAM

*Core Guidelines for the
Self-Parenting Practitioner*

John K. Pollard, III

Health Communications, Inc.
Deerfield Beach, Florida

Publisher: Health Communications, Inc.
        3201 S.W. 15th Street
        Deerfield Beach, Florida 33442-8190

Once again I dedicate this, my second book on
Self-Parenting, to the memory of Max Freedom Long.
Without his perseverance and devotion to uncovering
the truths of Huna, without his lifetime of toil in
relative obscurity, without his willingness to persevere
despite the lack of financial reward, there would
be no SELF-PARENTING® Program today
for future generations to enjoy.

ACKNOWLEDGMENTS

Many people have shared their insight, wisdom and experience of the Self-Parenting process with me. Among those who have influenced this book directly, I would particularly like to acknowledge:

— The ongoing practitioners of the Westside Support Group
— The Book Party participants
— Dennis Gottlieb, Caroline May and Susan Harris for insightful advice, editing suggestions and support
— Minna Eva Stern for superlative editorial feedback and for her deep insight on the Self-Parenting Process
— Lily Moussa for her superlative support, encouragement and management of the SELF-PARENTING Program.

To those listed above as well as to the readers of my first book, *SELF-PARENTING: The Complete Guide to Your Inner Conversations,* I appreciate your continuing feedback and support of the SELF-PARENTING® Program. Your contributions will enhance the future of many thousands of practitioners.

CONTENTS

FOREWORD

I am very excited about this book. First of all, I have already begun using much of the information it contains in my own Self-Parenting sessions, and as a result I have experienced a major improvement in the quality of my sessions. Secondly, the book is going to make my job as manager of the SELF-PARENTING Program much easier. It provides background information and instruction on virtually every problem that comes up in our workshops, seminars and consultations.

Working with the SELF-PARENTING Program and having the opportunity to work closely with its founder and creator have provided me with a knowledge and understanding that would be impossible to share with you in a few short paragraphs. However, I would like to take this opportunity to give you a brief look into the world of John Pollard.

Something many people do not know about John Pollard is that Self-Parenting is not his only area of expertise. He is also an expert bodyworker and healer, he is a pioneer in computer programming and animation, and he has developed a brilliant and highly original organization of human relationships.

One thing I've learned in my three years of working with John is that it would be impossible to actually "know" him in one lifetime. His wisdom, spirit and fountain of knowledge could only come from a man who has lived many more lifetimes than the one we all share now. I have witnessed John work in many seminar situations and on the telephone, and I am ever amazed at his ability to answer a question or deal with a problem that someone has had for weeks, months or years in just a sentence or a word. Perhaps his most amazing trait is that he is a man who practices what he preaches.

Personally, the SELF-PARENTING Program has touched my life in many dramatic ways. I am no longer a person who lives in a fantasy world 100 percent of the time just trying to escape reality. Now I am a person who lives in the "real world" and is actually living her dreams instead of just dreaming them. There are thousands of ways that the SELF-PARENTING Program has enriched and made a positive impact on my life. I know it can do the same for you.

I hope that you consider owning this book a privilege and that you will practice as an Inner Parent to apply the principles it presents as closely as possible. If you do, I can promise that your Self-Parenting style will improve dramatically and so will the experience of your Inner Child and Inner Parent.

Lily Moussa
Director, SELF-PARENTING Program

1

YOU HAVE A SELF-PARENTING STYLE

The Problem

Although everyone is naturally engaged in the Self-Parenting process, most people are unaware of this interaction occurring in their minds. This means you are likely to be neglecting or abusing your Inner Child by way of a negative Self-Parenting style without even knowing it.

The Solution

By paying attention to the continuous stream of your Inner Conversations, you will become more aware of your Inner Parent and Inner Child speaking to each other. Through the practice of daily half-hour sessions as an Inner Parent, you can learn how to change any negative styles of Self-Parenting to positive patterns. This way, rather than neglecting or abusing this precious part of you, you can learn to love, support and nurture your Inner Child's needs on a daily basis.

WHAT IS SELF-PARENTING?

Any explanation that attempts to define the process of Self-Parenting must begin with what are called "Inner Conversations." These are the constant mental communications or internal dialogues that occur just below the level of your conscious awareness. Everyone has Inner Conversations. They are as normal a part of human experience as eating, sleeping or breathing, and they affect every single aspect of daily life.

You have Inner Conversations every waking moment, even if you are not aware of them or try not to listen. Your mind continuously processes thoughts and feelings as part of your internal awareness. Some people are even afraid to tell others about these conversations inside their mind because they might be considered "crazy." Not only are Inner Conversations quite normal, they are the key to your happiness because the way you think and feel always originates within your Inner Conversations.

Self-Parenting is a paradigm that explains the characteristic interaction between the two voices having conversations inside your mind. These voices, called the Inner Parent and the Inner Child, talk to each other on a minute-to-minute basis. Each voice is a separate and distinct personality with its own character and moods. If you try writing out your own Inner Conversations, as have many thousands of Self-Parenting practitioners, you will see your own Inner Parent and Inner Child in action.

Your Inner Parent

Your Inner Parent is the internal voice that comes from the programming you received from your parents (or parental caretakers) between birth and age seven. As an infant you internalized without censorship the thoughts and emotional dynamics of your caretakers. Right or wrong, you absorbed their attitudes about life and adopted them as your own. Gradually you began testing and using what you learned by speaking and interacting with others. What you learned as a child became the mental voice responsible for directing your life through rational thinking and decision-making. Today your Inner Parent continues the role that your outer parents played in real life.

Your Inner Child

Your Inner Child's voice is the other major part of your personality. As a child you had an individual self, your emotional core, which you still retain today as a childlike personality inside your mind. This is a completely separate personality, one that contains the enthusiasm, needs and desires you had as a child. Your Inner Child represents the same feelings you had as a child, even though you are now an adult.

You experience happiness through the pleasures and joys of your Inner Child in the same way that parents enjoy life through their outer children. Your Inner Child's voice has as much impact on your personality and happiness right now as it did when you were a child.

Self-Parenting

Self-Parenting is the mental/emotional process of parenting yourself within your Inner Conversations. For better or for worse, your Inner Parent is parenting your Inner Child inside your mind in exactly the same way you were parented as a child. What most people consider to be the experience of thinking and feeling is more properly understood as the interaction or exchange between their Inner Parent and Inner Child. Each person has these two voices interacting inside the mind.

The influence your outer parents had on you was profound. As a child you mimicked your parents down to the last detail. You didn't have any choice because this process is biologically programmed. For example, researchers have repeatedly shown that children treat their dolls in a manner similar to the way their parents treat them. What hasn't been made clear until now is that you treat the Inner Child inside your mind in exactly the same way you were treated as a child.

Your Self-Parenting Style

The way your Inner Parent parents your Inner Child inside your Inner Conversations is called your "Self-Parenting style." Since you are automatically parenting yourself inside your mind, you automatically have a Self-Parenting style. The quality of your Self-Parenting style can be evaluated as being generally positive or generally negative, depending on the way your Inner Parent meets the physical, emotional, mental and social needs of your Inner Child.

Your parents (or significant others) gave you your Self-Parenting style. You learned what you were exposed to. The way you were taught to love, support and nurture your Inner Child was by mimicking, copying or adapting the way you were loved, supported and nurtured by others as a child. If your outer parenting was mostly positive, you are one of the fortunate few. If your outer parenting was mostly negative, then you will have to develop positive Self-Parenting skills as an Inner Parent to change from a negative to a positive Self-Parenting style.

Most people, having had a combination of positive and negative outer parenting, have a similar mixture of positive and negative Self-Parenting traits. Because they are not tuning in to their Inner Conversations, most people are unaware of the negative patterns associated with their Inner Parent. This creates a negative Self-Parenting style because such a person is not being responsive to the physical, emotional, mental and social needs of their Inner Child.

You don't have to be resigned to a negative Self-Parenting style if that is what you were given. This book sets forth a systematic method for developing a positive Self-Parenting style. If you are willing to practice the daily half-hour sessions, you can make amazing changes in the way that your Inner Parent treats your Inner Child. Always remember, however, that only you, as the Inner Parent, can make lasting changes in your Self-Parenting style. Other people cannot make these changes for you.

The SELF-PARENTING® Program

The SELF-PARENTING® Program is a system developed to enable you to learn about and change the dynamics of your Self-Parenting style. This system is described in detail in my first book, *SELF-PARENTING: The Complete Guide to Your Inner Conversations*. That book contains a complete description of the Inner Parent and Inner Child as well as many classic examples of how your Inner Conversations work. Part III of *SELF-PARENTING* contains a workbook section which presents the systematic process for opening up the communication between the two Inner Selves. The beginning procedures for these sessions are clearly described and a 14-day series of beginning questions is provided.

Daily half-hour sessions are the most important aspect of the SELF-PARENTING Program. During your beginning half-hour sessions you sit down as the Inner Parent and ask your Inner Child basic "getting to know you" questions. As the Inner Child responds, you write down each answer just as if you were speaking with a friend or doing an interview. Your Inner Child gets to say exactly what it wants without any interference or negativity from the Inner Parent. As you continue practicing the sessions, advanced techniques and methods can be learned to bring out your Inner Child.

For most people half-hour sessions with their Inner Child represent a significant renewal in their lives. As you become familiar with the half-hour format, your daily sessions with your Inner Child can be used for more active processes such as building self-esteem, establishing motivation for goals and deciding your future together. The methods of the SELF-PARENTING Program are also designed to solve "real world" issues such as weight problems, unhappiness, loneliness, job-related stress, school problems or relationship conflicts.

Why This Book Was Written

This book is a continuation, or more properly an expansion, of the principles and practices introduced in *SELF-PARENTING: The Complete Guide To Your Inner Conversations*. Students from around the world have read *SELF-PAR-*

ENTING and are actively learning how to love, support and nurture their Inner Child using the Self-Parenting half-hour format. Many thousands of people now recognize that Self-Parenting is the key to their Inner Conversations. This book is built around the typical questions and experiences most readers will have during the practice of daily half-hour sessions of Self-Parenting from two months to two years.

The challenge of changing your Self-Parenting style from negative to positive can be demanding in terms of the personal time and personal energy required. Still, the potential for improving your life will be worth the investment of time needed.

This book will:
- Encourage and motivate you to practice your 30-minute sessions with concentration and enthusiasm.
- Enable you, as an Inner Parent, to become more nurturing of your Inner Child.
- Help you to clarify "which voice is which" in your written Inner Conversations and Inner Conflicts.
- Guide you on the standards of positive Self-Parenting and expand upon the procedures outlined in *SELF-PARENTING: The Complete Guide to Your Inner Conversations.*
- Give you much advanced material for integration and discussion in Self-Parenting support groups.

To transform your Self-Parenting style over a period of time requires a firm commitment to half-hour Self-Parenting sessions every day for at least one year. You can easily and gently change your Self-Parenting style from negative to positive if you are willing to dedicate this time to practicing your half-hour sessions.

Self-Parenting is a tool. Self-Parenting does not make your life better by itself. You make your own life better by setting the principles of Self-Parenting into action within your own Inner Conversations. This book is for people who want to improve their Self-Parenting style using the techniques and practices created by the SELF-PARENTING Program. It offers invaluable insights through a series of essays and observations on the Self-Parenting process gathered during 20 years of investigating and teaching the process.

YOUR SELF-PARENTING STYLE

Creating a conscious, positive Self-Parenting style is the key to your personal happiness. Practicing the SELF-PARENTING Program can improve your life far beyond what you consider possible right now. There is only one catch: You must be willing to make the investment of 30 minutes on a daily basis to practice your Self-Parenting sessions. These pages will provide you with much intellectual information. However, if you don't practice the half-hour sessions, you won't be integrating this practical knowledge into your Self-Parenting style.

You begin by paying attention to what your Inner Parent and Inner Child are actually saying to each other. Then, as a practitioner of the SELF-PARENTING Program, you spend 30 minutes each day interacting directly with your Inner Child. By following a prescribed format and method of interaction, these sessions improve the quality of the relationship between your Inner Parent and Inner Child.

Changing your Self-Parenting style is a gentle process which you cannot force. You must proceed one session at a time, accumulating sessions over weeks and months. Part of the problem is, how can you change what you don't know you are doing? This is where the session format comes in. It takes many months of half-hour sessions to discover some of the deeper ways you, as the Inner Parent, are being negative to your Inner Child.

If you are not practicing half-hour sessions on a daily basis, you are missing one of the true values of life. The positive side effects of your half-hour sessions spill over into the "real world" in ways you cannot imagine. Simply by practicing these sessions in the prescribed manner, you will become more loving, supporting and nurturing as an Inner Parent. Half-hour sessions are a powerful method for reprogramming your Self-Parenting style.

The combined power of your Inner Parent and Inner Child is much stronger than that of your individual selves working alone. Although the time spent practicing daily sessions represents less than five percent of your time awake, what you learn about yourself during your sessions will more than exceed your insights during the rest of the day.

The Value of a Positive Self-Parenting Style

A positive Self-Parenting style will:
- Surprise you mentally and emotionally, as well as fill you with unexpected happiness.
- Evoke extraordinary feelings of personal tenderness and pathos.
- Introduce you to subtle patterns of personal energy that you have never before experienced and cannot experience in any other way.
- Remove the scarring and inflexibility from your cognitive process and replace them with discipline and personal freedom.
- Build a stable foundation for your success and achievements in life.

When you love, support and nurture your Inner Child:
- Your outer relationships improve.
- You will radiate happiness.
- You will become more organized.
- You will learn to let go and relax.
- Your communication skills will soar.
- You will become more assertive and confident, thus increasing your self-esteem.
- You will reduce your dependency on outer stimuli to fill emotional emptiness.

You will also find that the skills you use in your sessions will serve you in outer relationships as well. For example, you will:
- Listen more completely to your boss, co-workers and friends.
- Solve outer conflicts with fewer hassles.
- Express your thoughts and feelings more clearly.

There are many generic benefits to the daily practice of Self-Parenting sessions. The question is, which of these many benefits are going to mean the most to you?

There has been a tendency to misinterpret the scope and methods of Self-Parenting. The true purpose behind the SELF-PARENTING Program is to *retrain the Inner Parent.* Many people have perceived Self-Parenting as a way to "get in touch" with their Inner Child and mistakenly assume that it is the same as "Inner Child work." Although this observation appears true on the surface, the true focus of the SELF-PARENTING Program is to teach you how to become a more positive Inner Parent. Self-Parenting is "Inner Parent work," not "Inner Child work."

Beginning practitioners of the Self-Parenting Program often want to change the negative behavior of their Inner Child, behavior which they created in the first place! When the negative Inner Parent uses one of its typical negative methods to change the Inner Child, the Inner Child defends itself by creating even more rebellious behavior. Of course, this just makes the situation worse and eventually the Inner Parent is forced to give up.

Most people don't understand their Inner Child and how it responds to a negative Inner Parent. When your Inner Child is treated with abuse or neglect by your Inner Parent, it often responds with negative behavior. This behavior or "acting out" by your Inner Child is a reaction to the negative Self-Parenting style of your Inner Parent. It is not a part of the true personality of your Inner Child. Yet from the Inner Parent's point of view, the Inner Child seems to be the negative one.

For example, suppose your Inner Parent keeps telling lies to your Inner Child. Your Inner Child has the right to become angry and frustrated. If it becomes angry enough, it may even sabotage the Inner Parent. As a result, your Inner Parent may complain that the Inner Child is not cooperating. What is actually happening is that your Inner Child is being forced to use the misguided tactics of resistance or sabotage to seek attention and nurturing. Unfortunately, these types of negative behavior are the only ways your Inner Child knows to attempt meeting its needs.

When this happens, people want to practice Self-Parenting because their Inner Child is "out of control" or "running their lives." They are unhappy with the lows they are experiencing, and they want to change or manipulate their Inner Child in order to feel better. Some people have even said, "I don't like my Inner Child. How do I get a new one?"

Actually you, as the Inner Parent, will never be able to replace your Inner Child. You simply do not have that option. But suppose that somehow you could call the SELF-PARENTING Program and order a brand new, fresh and positive Inner Child. If you didn't change the Self-Parenting style of your Inner Parent, in a matter of a few weeks you would be experiencing the same negative behaviors from your "new" Inner Child that you had with the "old" one.

The purpose of the SELF-PARENTING Program is not to *change* the Inner Child. With the SELF-PARENTING Program, you learn to love, support and nurture your Inner Child to such a degree that it *evolves* into a completely positive personality—full of fun, love and energy.

Creating a positive Self-Parenting style will short-circuit this endless loop of negativity. Our method of changing the negative behavior of the Inner Child is to change the negative Self-Parenting style of the Inner Parent. This automatically lets the Inner Child feel better and become more positive. By changing the Inner Parent, the Inner Child automatically becomes more positive.

Half-hour sessions of Self-Parenting give the Inner Child positive attention and consideration of its needs. These sessions are often the first time the Inner Parent has ever paid attention to the Inner Child. As both selves experience the benefits of this practice within their sessions, they improve their relationship outside the sessions. Eventually, the greater part of their daily communication becomes positive and healthy.

What Kind of Inner Child Do You Have?

Is your Inner Child suppressed and withdrawn? Is it afraid to venture out into life? Do you have trouble creating the energy or motivation to achieve your goals? Is your Inner Child out of control? Are you involved constantly in addictive behavior? Do you spend every dime you make and then some? Are you eating, drinking or exercising yourself into the hospital? Are you forever doing battle with your Inner Child?

Your Inner Child affects your life in more ways than you may realize. Everything you want to achieve in life requires the cooperation of your Inner Child. It is the source of your energy and enthusiasm. The value of the Self-Parenting Program is that if you do a positive job as an Inner Parent, your Inner Child will automatically be enthusiastic and will want to help you.

What Kind of Inner Child Do You Want?

Your Inner Child could be spiteful, lonely or antisocial. Or it could be contented, happy and joyful. Physical or emotional excesses, such as overeating, sexual promiscuity and gambling, are examples of an "Inner Child gone wild." Yes, the Inner Child is out of control, but whose fault is it and what can you do about it? At worst, your Inner Child is an immature personality that needs love, proper guidance and teaching to mature. If the Inner Parent is not "present" to support the Inner Child, your Inner Child will be forced to seek a substitute form of behavior to try and meet its needs.

What Kind of Inner Parent Are You?

Are you positive and strong as an Inner Parent or are you negative and weak? Do you take the time to love, support and nurture your Inner Child each day, or do you unconsciously abuse and neglect your Inner Child? Do you struggle endlessly with your Inner Child, or would you like to work together in harmony?

As this book unfolds you are going to learn that the SELF-PARENTING Program always holds the Inner Parent responsible for the negative reactions and behavior of the Inner Child. You can't blame an immature child for running into the street, eating all the ice cream in the freezer or ripping up a $100 bill. You could predict that an unattended child might eat as much ice cream as it could and leave the rest to melt. A child is simply not mature enough to know better. Your Inner Child is like a younger family member who must be guided, rather than a spoiled brat who must be controlled.

If you, as the Inner Parent, have abandoned your Inner Child and provided nothing but negative guidance or a poor example, what other kinds of behavior can you expect? You will have excess in every form, as much as your Inner Child can get away with. Your Inner Child will act out this excessive behavior to the dismay and frustration of you, the Inner Parent.

The daily interactions you had with your early caretakers created your current Self-Parenting style. They taught you how to behave. You needed them to teach you values and proper behavior. Every child brought into this world was once a sweet, loving and innocent baby. If it later becomes an overeater, a gambler or a gang member terrorizing the streets, it was the parental environment of neglect and abuse that created this condition.

Your memories of childhood before the age of seven are mostly vague. You have largely forgotten your daily experiences other than a few major incidents. If your parents were loving, supporting and nurturing people, you were one of the lucky few.

For example, can you remember the 20 things your mother told you about school before the first grade? No? Well, these comments are still a part of how your Inner Parent feels about school and education at this very moment. How about the first 15 times you went to the doctor? What about what your mother said the time you forgot your lunch? As a child you were involved in hundreds of daily interactions that shaped your Inner Parent.

There is one additional factor to consider if you experienced negative outer parenting. Your Inner Child will have already established a negative pattern of coping and reacting to negative authority figures and/or negative life situations. You may discover through Self-Parenting that your Inner Child has been abandoned for quite a long time now. If this is true of your childhood, then it will take a determined effort on the part of your Inner Parent to reverse it.

It takes years to internalize your Self-Parenting pattern, but once internalized, it becomes functionally autonomous. This means your style or pattern of Self-Parenting your Inner Child becomes automatic and unconscious.

Because your day-in, day-out parental interactions created your Self-Parenting style, it will take many conscious half-hour sessions week-in and week-out to replace your negative Self-Parenting patterns with new, positive methods.

When you first begin practicing the SELF-PARENTING Program, most of your early sessions are designed simply to make you more aware of what you are thinking and feeling. This alone will help you immeasurably. Then, once your awareness has increased, you can use the material in this book to begin the advanced work of changing your negative Self-Parenting patterns to positive. Your Inner Child is present, waiting and wanting to be loved, but for the most part your Inner Parent is abusing or neglecting it. It may take many half-hour sessions of positive Self-Parenting before you can begin to uncover some of the more subtle ways you are hurting your Inner Child as a negative Inner Parent.

THE ORIGIN OF A NEGATIVE SELF-PARENTING STYLE

Children are created and managed physically, emotionally, mentally and socially by their parents. As children approach adulthood, they learn to take their place in society and assume responsibility for their own lives. Unfortunately, if children are exposed to negative outer parenting while they are young, they will carry a negative Self-Parenting style into adulthood. If they don't do anything to reverse this condition as adults, they will instill their negative Self-Parenting patterns into the next generation of children. This is how a negative Self-Parenting style can affect multiple generations.

The primary cause of a negative Self-Parenting style is a history of negative outer parenting. Although dysfunctional parenting has been a part of mankind from the beginning of time, only recently has this problem come into widespread social awareness. Public and social pressures are finally being brought to bear on parents who are physically or emotionally abusive, drug or alcohol addicted, or who mistreat their children in various other ways. We also have new social phenomena such as latch-key children, lack of day-care facilities and more single-parent families. These and other conditions of modern society combine to create a difficult environment for children who are dependent upon their parents for support.

This book is not about the prevalence of dysfunctional parenting in society; it is about reversing its effects—the widespread phenomenon of people with a negative Self-Parenting style. Whatever its cause, the direct consequence of negative outer parenting is a child who reaches adulthood with a negative Self-Parenting style. This individual will have an Inner Parent and Inner Child who are continually unhappy and in conflict with life.

Your Inner Parent Is Responsible

Every person has a Self-Parenting style. Based on the type of outer parenting you received, you will have a positive or negative Self-Parenting style. If your Self-Parenting style is fairly positive, you will find that your half-hour sessions rapidly enhance your already positive relationship with your Inner Child.

If your Self-Parenting style is negative, reversing the effects of dysfunctional parenting will take some time to uncover your patterns of negative parenting and to establish positive techniques to replace them. Practicing the half-hour sessions of the SELF-PARENTING Program consistently is an important part of this process.

If you experienced negative parenting as a child, the way you treat yourself now inside your mind is not your fault. You trusted your adult figures, and you wanted to be just like them so much so that you copied everything they said and did. You felt this was the way you were supposed to be when you grew up. You didn't know you were creating a negative Self-Parenting style at the time. But now as an adult you are stuck with what you were given. Your Self-Parenting style has become your responsibility.

If you don't have control of your Inner Conversations, who does? Although you are subject to external social and political influences, ultimately you are responsible for the internal response you have to these outside conditions. Even if your Inner Child feels gutsy enough to take the leadership role for the two selves, it simply isn't equipped to do so.

Your Inner Parent has the responsibility of leadership within your Self-Parenting relationship. If the Inner Parent doesn't lead, your Inner Child can't follow. The Inner Parent may try to discuss or rationalize itself out of this responsibility. It may even choose to ignore this reality as a form of denial. However, the leadership role of the Inner Parent cannot be changed. Eventually, as this awareness sinks in, the Inner Parent can redirect its energy from avoiding responsibility toward creating positive interaction between the two Inner Selves. This process requires energy on the part of the Inner Parent, but the reward is great.

Remember, your Inner Child is the *only* personality which you, the Inner Parent, can be absolutely certain of being in a relationship with at all times and for the rest of your life. You and your Inner Child are in a relationship for as long as you live. As the Inner Parent you could avoid this responsibility inside your mind and still be relatively successful in the outer world. You may know of individuals who have all the trappings of outer success, yet are still unhappy with their lives because of their negative Inner Conversations.

Ideally at some point you, as the Inner Parent, will truly realize that you and the Inner Child are in a permanent and significant relationship. As a result you will resolve to make your relationship happy, productive and everything that a positive relationship can be. Ultimately, you are the one who benefits. YOU! No one else can help you here. Your initiative alone will ensure your success. If you are unhappy with your life, you, as the Inner Parent, are the one who is responsible for making it better.

The Qualities of the Positive Inner Parent

The potential strengths of your Inner Parent are the same strengths that the ideal outer parent would have. Your Inner Parent can be an excellent teacher, providing guidance and setting examples for your Inner Child. Your Inner Parent can maintain an intimate sense of caring and support for your Inner Child so that it develops its own talents and skills. When you express positive concern for your Inner Child or give it encouragement, you are voicing the positive Inner Parent.

During times of stress the positive Inner Parent is a calming, soothing voice that is always present to help and support your Inner Child. The Inner Parent makes decisions, chooses options and evaluates priorities for both Inner Selves. The positive Inner Parent will support and nurture the Inner Child when it is scared or angry by asking the Inner Child what its needs are and providing them. The positive Inner Parent can provide the Inner Child with whatever it wants or needs by practicing the SELF-PARENTING Program. Training and experience allow the positive Inner Parent to become highly developed in rational thinking and intellectual activity.

The positive Inner Parent provides stability and support for the Inner Child by being nurturing and loving during Self-Parenting sessions with the Inner Child. Part of this process is achieved by the elimination of negative behavior by the Inner Parent. The other part comes from beginning to activate a positive Self-Parenting style within your Inner Conversations.

The Negative Inner Parent

The negative Inner Parent is susceptible to the same weaknesses of neglectful and non-nurturing behavior that your outer parents might have used. Your Inner Parent can be quick to judge and lecture your Inner Child. It is common for it to warn, advise or berate the feelings of the Inner Child. Many times your Inner Parent will make a major life decision without even asking your Inner Child how it feels, just as your outer parents did to you as a child.

While being intellectual may be the Inner Parent's strong suit, this can also lead to some serious errors in judgment. In other words, the Inner Parent can act irrationally at times and make human mistakes. It can also be petty and nit-picking. It is the "should" side of the Inner Conversation, tending to be the voice that says "you should do this" and "you shouldn't do that." It can also be an overly critical and threatening voice. The negative traits you were exposed to while being parented are apt to be part of your Self-Parenting style.

Your Inner Parent has a major position of influence over your Inner Child and is likely to be the voice that you hear the loudest and longest in your Inner Conversations. If your Inner Parent does not nurture your Inner Child, your joy and enthusiasm for life will be missing. Unless both Inner Selves are happy within your Inner Conversations, neither self will be happy.

Have you ever heard new parents say they have no intention of making the same mistakes with their children that their parents made with them? Later they find themselves repeating verbatim the words and actions of their own parents. The reason is that these negative statements from their parents have become part of their deeper Self-Parenting style. As you become more and more experienced with your half-hour sessions, you will realize you are still being treated and guided as if by your parents. Only now you are doing it to yourself, all by yourself, within your Inner Conversations.

The negative Inner Parent often neglects, invalidates, misunderstands or completely ignores the needs and desires of the Inner Child. It can abuse its Inner Child by being selfish and demanding or by being too much of a perfectionist and putting undue pressure on the Inner Child. If your outer parents did a poor job of nurturing and loving you during your childhood, you will tend toward non-nourishing and negative Self-Parenting.

Self-Parenting and ACA Issues

Possibly the most complete portfolios of dysfunctional and abusive outer parenting belong to a group of people known collectively as Adult Children of Alcoholics. This group was formed in the mid-1980s as an offshoot of the Alcoholics Anonymous (AA) and Al-Anon 12-Step programs. Although it is certainly not their fault, ACAs have Self-Parenting styles that are necessarily some of the worst on record.

ACAs have it tough. Outer parents with alcohol or other chemical addictions are unable to meet the needs of their children because maintaining their own chemical dependencies is too all-consuming an activity. Also, the frequency of arguments and the levels of tension in such a household can be even more upsetting to the child than the parent's abusive treatment. These factors translate directly to the ACA's Self-Parenting style.

ACAs did not have a positive role model for outer parenting. For example, holidays are supposed to be warm, happy, sharing times of love and communion with family. Yet holidays often represent the periods of greatest family stress for ACAs. Alcoholic parents often use the holidays as an excuse for non-stop drinking. Parents who are distant and neglectful of their children often make this painfully clear at Christmas time. One year, a Self-Parenting student received an expensive chemistry set from his parents that he remembers hating and which he never used. The following year he received the exact same present from his parents.

Parents who suffer from alcohol or chemical addictions create children who grow up to be adults who:

- Suppress spontaneity
- Do not talk openly about their experiences or feelings
- Feel inadequate, tense or upset for no reason
- Deny, repress or block out their emotions
- Feel empty and/or unhappy without knowing why
- Feel anxious and worried for no apparent reason
- Are suspicious of warmth, caring, trust, freedom, choice or negotiation
- Are distrustful of others

The interesting consequence is that each of these conditions is the direct result of negative outer parenting on the person's Inner Child. Findings now indicate that these unfortunate patterns are passed down through generations. And of course these negative emotions remain within the person's Inner Child through adulthood. As a result, through no fault of their own, ACAs carry forward the same negative parenting dynamics into their Inner Conversations whether they drink alcohol or not. The same tension levels that existed within their family interactions become entrenched as part of the ACA's Self-Parenting style.

Prior to the formation of this 12-Step program, most ACAs lived in their own private shame, putting up a good front but feeling crippled emotionally. In 1985, brave souls all over America began meeting together and sharing their common experiences with dysfunctional parenting. By this time the ACAs had clearly established "The Problem." They knew the goal was to "Become Your Own Loving Parent," although they had no direct or practical methods to accomplish this purpose. Even though the 12-Step program of AA presents an excellent solution for those who need immediate help with alcohol problems, it was never designed to acknowledge or repair a dysfunctional Self-Parenting style.

My heart goes out to ACAs. Although their secrets are finally coming to light, they must work hard to relearn a positive Self-Parenting style. The good news is that all their hard work will be rewarded many times over, as many case histories have shown. To their credit, ACAs and their therapists were the first people as a group to recognize and validate the importance of the SELF-PARENTING Program.

Unfortunately, regardless of *why* outer parents were dysfunctional, children from this type of family background will have a dysfunctional Self-Parenting style. Many people who think they have completely changed their Self-Parenting style, through various meditation or personal growth techniques, find out after starting Self-Parenting sessions that they have only changed its most superficial aspects. They may have changed *what* their Inner Parent was saying or doing, but not *the way* it was saying and doing it.

For example, one practitioner suffered horribly from parents who were religious fundamentalists. Once she escaped from their influence, she joined a new religion and took a "completely different" approach to life. But without realizing it, her Inner Parent continued the identical style of abusing her Inner Child, using the new religious tenets. She unknowingly repeated the same negative Self-Parenting style her parents had given her, substituting the new words and ideas into her old Self-Parenting style. Until she began Self-Parenting sessions, she never realized what she was doing to her Inner Child.

Another interesting phenomenon is that many parents who have become aware of their ACA backgrounds made a herculean effort to parent their outer children in a positive manner. They worked overtime to ensure that they did not repeat on their outer children the patterns of parenting they received. Yet, despite their success as outer parents, they still continue to practice a negative Self-Parenting style on their own Inner Child.

Thankfully, now something can be done to reverse these unfortunate patterns of abuse and neglect. As conscious and free-thinking adults, people who have suffered from dysfunctional outer parenting can change the negative Self-Parenting habits they were given by others and replace them with positive Self-Parenting. Even if this process takes several months, they will begin to notice remarkable changes in the way they think and feel. *The only thing separating the experience of ACAs from the rest of us is their awareness of the problem. Almost everyone will have at least some aspects of a negative Self-Parenting style that are holding them back in life.*

CHANGING YOUR INNER PARENT

The relationship you have with your Inner Child is the most important relationship you will ever have. The Inner Parent/Inner Child relationship takes place throughout your lifetime; there is no divorce or being fired from your Inner Child. One feature of the Self-Parenting relationship is that you will always maintain your role as the Inner Parent. You cannot decide one day to let your Inner Child be the Inner Parent for a few months.

You cannot silence your Inner Child; you cannot tell your feelings to go away. Trying to do so will have a deeply negative effect on your personality. Although you cannot control your Inner Child, except temporarily perhaps, this doesn't stop the typical Inner Parent from trying. These attempts take many forms. Ignoring or discounting your feelings is one example; rationalizing them is another.

Suppressing the voice of your Inner Child will not eliminate it from the picture. In fact, suppression of your Inner Child is a Lose/Lose situation all the way. First of all, it takes a tremendous amount of mental willpower and energy to hold down your Inner Child. The energy and concentration this takes is similar to trying to hold a beach ball under water. The deeper you push the ball, the more energy it takes and the more likely the ball is to pop out of the water. Using energy to suppress your Inner Child only depletes your Inner Parent's meager reserves. The Inner Child also loses by not feeling accepted and not being able to channel its energy creatively.

People deny reality in order to avoid painful truths. But denying the physical perceptions of what your Inner Child sees, hears, touches, tastes or smells is a mistake. The Inner Child is connected to the five senses. It is the self that physically sees, hears, touches, tastes, and smells. The painful reality you are trying to deny won't go away. It will just bury itself deeper within your Inner Conversations.

The SELF-PARENTING Program defines denial as an Inner Parent who tries to deny the physical experiences of its Inner Child. Suppose your Inner Child is experiencing physical or emotional abuse as the result of someone's behavior. It represents denial when the Inner Parent attempts to rationalize this behavior as acceptable. Because your Inner Child represents the physical senses, it still sees, hears and feels abused so it doesn't accept your rationalizing. Denial of your Inner Child's experiences is one of the first negative behaviors to disappear after you begin Self-Parenting sessions.

The Inner Parent may not want to accept the feelings of the Inner Child. It may be afraid of these feelings for various reasons. Or your Inner Parent may attempt to change or make excuses for these emotions of the Inner Child. The more you practice half-hour sessions, the more you become aware of your patterns of communication with your Inner Child. If your pattern has been to manipulate your Inner Child with lies and promises you never keep, your Inner Child will quickly let you know how it feels about that!

As you become more aware of your Self-Parenting style, you also become more sensitive to the experience of truth from your Inner Child. If you try to pretend with your Inner Child, you will lose its trust. You can be dishonest anywhere else and with anyone else, but within your Inner Conversations you cannot lie. If you discover this pattern within yourself, you must change it as soon as possible.

A good rule for the Inner Parent to keep with the Inner Child is, "Make a promise, keep a promise." By refusing to keep your promises to the Inner Child, you create tension and stress within your Inner Conversations. Your Inner Child is well aware when you make a promise that you don't keep. And it will never fully accept your rationalized explanations when you try to contradict that reality. The sooner you learn not to make promises you can't keep, the happier both of you will be. The sooner you learn to follow through when you give your Inner Child your word, the more fulfilled both of you will be. Once your Inner Child knows you are doing your best to be honest, it will trust you much more in the difficult situations.

Remember, if you have a problem with your Self-Parenting style, the responsibility lies with your Inner Parent. Your Inner Child is not the cause of your problems, although it may appear that way to a weak or lazy Inner Parent. Self-Parenting was not designed to change your Inner Child. Your goal is simply to love, support and nurture your Inner Child so much that it becomes positive and loving in return. As much as your half-hour sessions benefit the Inner Child, their true value is in the changes they create in the Self-Parenting style of the Inner Parent. Self-Parenting can benefit the Inner Parent as much as and even more than the Inner Child!

Keeping this in mind, we are going to begin improving your Self-Parenting style by looking at some of the key traits of positive and negative outer parenting. Examining these traits will enable you to recognize more easily the positive and negative aspects of your Self-Parenting style. You will begin to recognize negative aspects of your Self-Parenting style so that positive, ongoing Self-Parenting will be possible.

As you will see, most of the problems associated with a negative Self-Parenting style are the result of your Inner Parent neglecting or in some way abusing your Inner Child. It is the *reaction* by the Inner Child to this abuse or neglect that creates the initial problem for the Inner Parent. Your Inner Child's fighting or defensive reaction against this neglect or abuse is normal, even healthy. Once the Inner Parent cleans up its side of the Self-Parenting relationship, the Inner Child's negativity or "problem" disappears.

THE SELF-PARENTING INTERACTION

Now, as the Inner Parent, you are ready to cultivate deeper insights into your Inner Parent/Inner Child interactions. The SELF-PARENTING Program has established that all traits of negative Self-Parenting can be placed in one of two categories of behavior—neglect or abuse. Learning to place the many types of parenting traits into one of these two basic categories will help you recognize when you are making the same mistakes within your Inner Conversations.

These two general categories of negative Self-Parenting can most easily be recognized by relating them to the relationship between an outer parent and outer child. In this chapter we will explore how these outer parenting patterns become internalized into our Self-Parenting style by comparing the example of an outer parent/outer child exchange.

Neglect

Neglect is defined as:
- To ignore or not pay attention to
- To fail to care for or give proper attention to
- To not take care of, as through carelessness or oversight

The SELF-PARENTING Program uses the term *neglect* to represent all the possible types of "passive behaviors" of the outer parent that can hurt or injure the outer child. There are various forms of neglect such as withholding attention, ignoring the child's communications or abandoning the child emotionally. All these patterns of outer parenting create problems for the child, who is left with neither a direction to follow nor the discipline for sustained efforts.

Abuse

Abuse is defined as:
- To handle wrongly or improperly
- To hurt or injure by maltreatment
- To assail with contemptuous, coarse or insulting words

Abuse covers the "active behaviors" of the outer parent that can hurt or injure an outer child. Examples of this type of parenting would be beating a child, locking it in a closet, shouting or inflicting other types of physical or emotional damage.

Whether neglect or abuse, the effect on the child is still devastating; the child is physically, emotionally or mentally injured. Defining these two categories of behavior as passive or active helps to isolate and clarify the specific parental actions.

Let's examine a hypothetical outer parent/outer child exchange to explore an example of these two patterns in action. Imagine a parent and child traveling together for the first time to a large city. The child has lived in the country all her life (four years) and has never seen a tall building. When they get off the downtown bus the little girl (who has been asleep) sees a sky-scraper, becomes scared and asks:

"Mommy, Mommy, will that big house fall on me?"

The mother has essentially four possible responses to her child's question. Two reflect negative outer parenting and two represent positive outer parenting.

Negative Outer Parenting: Neglect

The outer parent could neglect or ignore her child's comment. This could be intentional or unintentional on the parent's part. Either way, the results are still the same. Perhaps a bus roared loudly by and the mother could not hear what her child said, or she was distracted by getting luggage. Perhaps the mother thought the child's comment so ignorant that she needn't acknowledge such a meaningless fear. Whatever the reason, the bottom line is that the parent does not acknowledge the child's communication. The outer parent either ignores or is not paying attention to the comments of her child, which constitutes the condition of neglect.

Negative Outer Parenting: Abuse

A negative exchange also occurs if the parent responds to her child's concerns with comments such as, "Shut up," "Don't be ridiculous," "You're silly," "How stupid can you get?" or "What an idiot." Perhaps she leans over and gives her child a swat for even asking the question. What the child receives for expressing her fears is criticism, belittlement or possibly even physical blows. This pattern is called abuse and is all too common in typical outer parent/outer child interactions.

Two other categories of behavior which reflect positive parenting could be taken by the parent. The first is paying attention. The second is responding appropriately. These two categories of behavior provide the natural antithesis of neglect and abuse.

Positive Outer Parenting: Paying Attention

Paying attention is defined as:
- Close or careful observation or listening
- Being attentive, noticing
- Granting consideration or courtesy

When *paying attention,* the parent is prepared to meet the needs of the child. Paying attention does much for the child by expressing acceptance and providing the security a child needs. Even if the mother simply looks at her child and smiles, the child registers this response and knows that it has been heard. If the mother listens to and acknowledges her child's comment without neglecting or abusing her, this is a positive parenting behavior.

Positive Outer Parenting: Responding Appropriately

A second possible action by the mother is to *respond appropriately* to the child. Responding appropriately can mean anything from simply listening to the child to answering its question or helping the child meet its needs. This involves one of three actions. The use of each option depends on the type of problem the child presents.

Responding appropriately means to take the action suitable to the state or condition of the child. In the SELF-PARENTING Program responding appropriately is based on:
  • Listening if the child is sharing an observation
  • Teaching if the child is asking a questior.
  • Supporting if the child is expressing a need

Responding appropriately is an advanced skill of positive parenting in that the parent must be paying enough attention to the child to then determine the purpose of the child's communication. These skills are not widely understood and were defined specifically by the SELF-PARENTING Program. Each particular skill of responding appropriately is discussed below.

Listen: If the Outer Child Is Sharing an Observation

Often a child will say something just for the sake of saying it. It may want to make an observation, offer an opinion or give its parents some information it thinks they might need. In this situation the outer parent's role is simply to be there, listen to the child and share the exchange. To experience that its communication matters to another gives the child a sense of identity, self-esteem and social standing.

Teach: If the Outer Child Is Asking a Question

Teaching is the major role of the outer parent. Children spend their childhood asking questions. After asking a question, the child gives rapt attention to the parent and trusts the parent implicitly; it believes everything it is told as gospel. This trust is part of the natural functioning of the parent/child relationship.

When the child asks a question, the positive parent uses this opportunity to teach or explain to the outer child. For example, in the situation mentioned above, the mother might use the following dialogue:

"Oh no, darling, the building won't fall down. You'll be okay. Those tall houses are called buildings and they are built by trained people called architects. They make sure the buildings are strong before they are built and that they won't fall down . . .."

Support: If the Outer Child Is Expressing a Need

Often the reason a child is communicating is to express a need. This subject is so important that an entire section of this book is devoted to the concept of defining and determining needs. In the present example, the child is bothered by a fear. She expresses this fear by asking her mother if the "big house" will fall on her.

Suppose instead that the child was sweltering hot and had a complaint, such as:

"Mommy, Mommy, the sun is too hot on my head."

In this case teaching wouldn't be very helpful for the child. Suppose the parent explained to the child:

"Yes, darling, the sun beats down from the sky and it's very warm and your little brow can get quite hot."

This bit of wisdom doesn't help the child very much.

In this situation the child is really expressing a need to cool off. The outer parent can fulfill its role in a positive manner by supporting or assisting the outer child to meet its needs. The outer parent responds appropriately to the child by wiping its forehead, providing the child with a hat or in some way making the child more comfortable. When the outer child wants to be more comfortable, less afraid or happier and is unable to do that for itself, it asks the parent to meet its needs.

Application to Your Self-Parenting Interactions

The Inner Parent has the identical role in the Inner Parent/Inner Child relationship as the outer parent in a outer parent/outer child relationship. The negative Inner Parent has the potential to neglect or abuse the Inner Child. The positive Inner Parent will pay attention to and respond appropriately to the Inner Child.

Your Inner Child has one of three goals when trying to communicate with you. It is either sharing a viewpoint, asking a question or expressing a need. You as the Inner Parent have the same four options of response as in the outer parent/child relationship. You respond to your Inner Child using one of these four styles of parenting hundreds of times each day within your Inner Conversations. Your Self-Parenting style depends on the number of times you:
- Neglect
- Abuse
- Pay attention to
- Respond appropriately to your Inner Child

If we could hook a computer up to your Inner Conversations, we would be able to print out each of the conversations between your Inner Parent and Inner Child. Based on the printout, we could determine the type of response your Inner Parent made to each communication by your Inner Child. Depending on the percentage of each category, your Self-Parenting style would be positive or negative.

As a hypothetical example, suppose your Inner Child communicated to you a thousand times in one day. As the Inner Parent you responded with:
- Neglect   460 times
- Abuse   230 times
- Paying attention to   300 times
- Responding appropriately to   10 times

You would have a negative Self-Parenting style for this day based on 690 negative responses and 310 positive responses as an Inner Parent.

If your chart looked like this:
- Neglect   125 times
- Abuse   95 times
- Paying attention to   463 times
- Responding appropriately to   317 times

then you would have a positive Self-Parenting style based on 220 negative responses and 780 positive responses.

Unfortunately, until we do have such computer capabilities, we are each left to determine the state of our Self-Parenting style the old-fashioned way, by writing out our Inner Conversations and determining the response pattern for ourselves. The majority of people we have worked with in the SELF-PARENTING Program have an overwhelmingly negative Self-Parenting style in the beginning.

Let's use a practical example to demonstrate the above principles of parental response in a Self-Parenting situation. Suppose you've gone shopping downtown. You didn't bring an umbrella and now it's beginning to rain. As you exit a store your Inner Child clearly suggests buying an umbrella so you won't get wet.

Negative Self-Parenting: Neglect

Neglect is most often the case within your Inner Conversations. When your Inner Child makes a comment or expresses a fear, your Inner Parent is either too busy, not paying attention or regards the comment as insignificant. Sadly, in many instances, your Inner Parent never hears the comments of your Inner Child because they take place below the conscious level of your awareness. Your Inner Child is thus left unheard and unacknowledged.

In this example, the thought ("Let's buy an umbrella") suggested by the Inner Child is never heard by the Inner Parent. He or she is so busy thinking about the next appointment or complaining about the rain that the Inner Child's message is never even received. The interesting thing is that this happens inside your own mind. No one else does this to you.

Negative Self-Parenting: Abuse

Your Inner Parent often subjects your Inner Child to mental abuse within your Self-Parenting interactions. Typically this abuse is of the same type and quality that your parents gave to you when you were growing up. Usually this is unconscious on your part, but it occurs nonetheless. As you become more aware of your Self-Parenting style, you will notice or hear your Inner Parent abusing your Inner Child in a manner that will surprise you.

What would happen if, after the Inner Child's suggestion, your Inner Parent automatically and unconsciously responded with:

"Don't be stupid. That's a dumb idea. We have a perfectly good umbrella at home. It's no big deal if we get wet."

In this example, instead of being heard and responded to appropriately, your Inner Child is attacked by the Inner Parent for bringing up a good idea. Granted, this might be considered mild abuse, but the pattern still exists. The situation could be pretty bad depending on how hard it's raining.

So how are the patterns of neglect and abuse reversed by the Inner Parent? By paying attention and responding appropriately.

Positive Self-Parenting: Paying Attention

Paying attention to the Inner Child is the first rule of the Inner Parent. If you are not aware of what your Inner Child is saying, how can you respond appropriately? This is the most troublesome area for the new practitioner to learn. You must be listening to your Inner Conversations to find out what your Inner Child is saying.

In our example, because the Inner Parent has been practicing daily half-hour sessions, it actually hears the Inner Child's suggestion to purchase an umbrella when exiting the store. As part of its normal day, the Inner Parent is beginning to recognize and pay attention to this voice inside.

Positive Self-Parenting: Responding Appropriately

The next step, after hearing what the Inner Child says, is to decide how to respond. Is the Inner Child sharing a general observation, asking a question or expressing a need? Based on what the Inner Child is communicating, there are three potential categories of response.

Listen: If Your Inner Child Is Sharing an Observation

The first consideration of the Inner Parent is to listen to the Inner Child. Many times the Inner Child just wants to contribute its opinion. When it makes a comment about a situation such as the rain, it simply wants to be heard and feel accepted. In these instances, listening and accepting what the Inner Child says are all you need to do to respond appropriately.

However, in this example listening is not enough. The Inner Child has made a suggestion and expects a response. Since the Inner Parent is listening to what the Inner Child has suggested, it must then consider the proposal.

Teach: If Your Inner Child Is Asking a Question

In our rain example, teaching is not called for. Both selves know it is raining and it's really not time for a lesson in meteorology. In order to respond appropriately, the Inner Parent must resolve the Inner Child's concern/fear or fulfill its need.

If your Inner Child is asking you a question, then the appropriate response is to find out the answer. Perhaps your Inner Child is wondering what your boss "really" said. Or it just saw a unique animal at the zoo that it wants to know more about. To respond appropriately as the Inner Parent, you must be willing to find the answer to your Inner Child's question and explain the answer.

Support: If Your Inner Child Is Expressing a Need

In this example our positive Inner Parent hears the suggestion of the Inner Child. It then carefully, if quickly, runs through the conditions of the situation mentally.

- "How hard is it raining?"
- "Is it going to get worse?"
- "How much are these street umbrellas?"
- "What clothes are we wearing and what happens if they get wet?"
- "How much did this suit cost?"
- "What else do we have to do today?"
- "Where is the car and how far do we have to walk to get there?"

These and other questions could be considered within a brief moment of your Inner Conversations. If it seemed like a good idea, maybe the Inner Parent would allow the purchase of the umbrella. If not, at least the Inner Child's comments were responded to appropriately and it doesn't feel slighted or ignored.

By becoming aware of the two negative and two positive Self-Parenting response options, you can begin observing the way you, as an Inner Parent, respond to your Inner Child within your Inner Conversations. Based on the understanding you gain, you will be able to start improving your Self-Parenting style almost immediately.

Your Inner Parent's Role in Self-Parenting

Your Inner Parent has the crucial role in the Self-Parenting relationship. Just as outer parents must keep a watchful eye on their children to anticipate and determine their children's needs, so you, as the Inner Parent, must do the same for your Inner Child. Part of your role within this process is to shape and guide the education of your Inner Child. As the Inner Parent, your goal is to discover the unique characteristics of your Inner Child and bring them out.

The only unsolvable problem within your Inner Conversations is if you, as the Inner Parent, refuse to become a positive Inner Parent. This creates within your Inner Child the feeling of being abandoned, divorced or fired.

Since you can never truly abandon, divorce or fire your Inner Child, you will simply be stuck with your negative feelings. If instead you accept the responsibility for your role as an Inner Parent, you can make your life full and satisfying and keep it that way.

Remember you are always responsible for the inner world of your thoughts and feelings. Every task you perform in life and every goal you want to achieve is first experienced through the process of your Inner Conversations. This includes such everyday experiences as going to the supermarket, buying clothes or doing the laundry. Decisions you consider such as planning your vacation, deciding who to marry and resolving career conflicts are based on your Self-Parenting interaction. Inner Conversations also take place concerning events that are purely external to your life, such as the weather, the economy or politics.

Your Inner Parent must accept the major responsibility for the internal workings of your Inner Conversations. Its overall duty is to internalize positive outer parenting skills into your half-hour sessions and Inner Conversations. The Inner Parent must make decisions, choose options, and evaluate priorities in your life. For best results you must do this with the cooperative input of your Inner Child. If you try to perform this function on your own, you may meet strong resistance and possibly even sabotage from your Inner Child.

The way the positive Inner Parent fulfills its role is to provide for the physical, emotional, mental and social needs of the Inner Child. The more aware you become of the individual quirks and personality of your Inner Child, the more you will be able to love, support and nurture this special part of you. Your Inner Child is as different from your Inner Parent as outer children are different from their outer parents. Your personal Inner Child has an individual temperament that you, as the Inner Parent, must take the time to know and understand.

Learning to understand and work with your Inner Child is not easy. After all, if it were, we would all be doing it. The first step, of course, is to become aware of the communication style between the two Inner Selves. Once you know how the two selves are communicating with each other, you can use your half-hour sessions to change any negative interactions to positive ones.

2

GUIDELINES FOR PRACTITIONERS

The Problem

Without a model for positive outer parenting, learning to become a positive Inner Parent is very difficult. The half-hour format for Self-Parenting sessions is easy to follow. However, if you inadvertently change the procedures, you will experience problems during your sessions. If you neglect this format, you will find it difficult to maintain daily sessions.

The Solution

Begin your practice of the SELF-PARENTING Program by following the correct format from the beginning. This session format is straightforward and easy to follow as well as being essential to protect your Inner Child from a negative Inner Parent. By following the format you will BE a positive Inner Parent as well as absorb the positive principles of the Self-Parenting Format into your daily life.

PRACTITIONER GUIDELINES

You are the most important person in your life. Not your father, not your mother, not your husband, not your wife, not your son, not your daughter, not your best friend. You are the most important thing in your life. Not your house, not your job, not your yard, not your hobby, not your money, not your car, not your hair, not your computer. So, when something as good for you as Self-Parenting comes along, take advantage of it.

To get the most value from the SELF-PARENTING Program, you must practice daily sessions in which you devote 30 minutes each day to the relationship with your Inner Child. This is the best way to take the abstract theory of Self-Parenting and put it into practice.

When you first begin Self-Parenting, you gain amazing benefits from what appears to be such an easy procedure. Simply by asking your Inner Child some basic questions, writing down the answers and saying, "Thank you, Inner Child, for telling me that," you gain a remarkable number of benefits. However, this ease of practice should not be taken lightly by the Inner Parent. If you alter these procedures, it is possible to experience difficulty when starting Self-Parenting.

Although the format of the SELF-PARENTING Program may be easy to follow, underneath its simplicity is a specific structure that is designed to protect your Inner Child from a more than likely negative Inner Parent. Every aspect of this structure is important. You should not change or alter this format if you want to receive the full benefits of the SELF-PARENTING Program.

It is virtually impossible for a person to become aware of their true Self-Parenting style until practicing sessions for at least three months. This discovery was a very important consideration in the design of the program. You will not receive the full benefits of practicing the SELF-PARENTING Program if you think that changing some aspect of it is "no big deal" because you heard about something similar once.

The first three months of Self-Parenting are just as important, maybe more so, for the Inner Parent as for the Inner Child. The Inner Parent is learning through practice how to become a positive Inner Parent. Remember, if you have had a particularly difficult or abusive childhood, chances are you have an abusive Inner Parent beneath your conscious awareness. The structure of the early sessions is designed to "muzzle" the negative Inner Parent.

The session format trains your Inner Parent how to ask your Inner Child a question and then listen to the answer, perhaps for the first time ever. Since your Inner Child is grateful for the attention, you will automatically become a positive Inner Parent if you follow the session guidelines properly. This does not mean that your Inner Child won't experience some emotional or cathartic feelings. Your early sessions could be filled with some very strong emotional feedback from your Inner Child.

The session format is designed to protect the Inner Child through any type of emotional circumstance. During the first three to six months of Self-Parenting there is a wide range of "normal" progress. Some people gain insights and understanding immediately that others might not get for several months, but within six months everyone begins to absorb the basic fundamentals of the Self-Parenting process. This is so because of the session format.

It is especially important that you, as the Inner Parent, don't subject your Inner Child to faulty practices during your early sessions. If you are one who has tried the program and felt that it didn't work as positively as you would have liked, you may have unknowingly altered the program in some way.

The following guidelines are the recommended procedures of the SELF-PARENTING Program. They answer the questions that most practitioners have asked concerning the practice of half-hour sessions. Once you have incorporated these procedures into an established routine, they become second nature.

Before Your Session

1. Practice your Self-Parenting sessions in the morning, right after you wake up. Anything later will dilute the value of your sessions. If this is difficult for you, keep in mind that *EVERYONE* who has switched to morning sessions has benefited immensely. Practicing sessions before you go to bed is definitely not recommended because sleeping dissipates the energy you have generated.

2. Record your sessions on ruled 8½ x 11 inch paper. Keep your sessions in a special binder used only for that purpose. Steno pads, loose sheets, or spiral notebooks are not as effective for this purpose. Three-hole punch any materials such as newsletters, modules or materials you receive from the SELF-PARENTING Program and keep these in your folder as well.

3. Before you start your session, write the day, date and time at the top of the page. This is when to start timing your session.

4. Use the left side of the page to record the Inner Parent's questions and the right side to record the Inner Child's responses. You may draw a line down the center of the paper to help guide you.

5. Always begin your session with "The Opening." This must be spoken *OUT LOUD* by your Inner Parent.

During Your Session

6. Ask each question *OUT LOUD.* When you ask the question, you must also write out the full question. *SPEAK AND WRITE THE WORDS AT THE SAME TIME.* Slowing down your speech to match your writing speed takes some practice, but it is worth it because this technique concentrates and clears your mind for the response of your Inner Child. This technique becomes even easier when you start making up your own questions.

7. *DROP DOWN TO THE NEXT LINE* on the paper when you begin writing the response of your Inner Child on the right-hand side of the page. This makes your sessions easier to read and analyze.

8. Write whatever your Inner Child says *EXACTLY AS IT SAYS IT.* Whatever your Inner Child's response — whether it is a one-word answer, a question, a complaint about doing the session or a scathing attack on you as the Inner Parent—write it down exactly.

9. After you have finished writing out the Inner Child's response, always reply *OUT LOUD* with, "Thank you, Inner Child, for telling me that." This response is crucial, no matter what the Inner Child says.

10. As you say "Thank you, Inner Child, for telling me that," make a note that you made this statement in the following manner. *DROP TO THE BEGIN-NING OF THE NEXT LINE* on the left side of the page and write the capital letters **TY** and circle them as you say the words out loud. This way you do not have to write out the words each time. As a result, before each new question by the Inner Parent on the left, there will be a circled **TY.**

11. Resist any temptation to respond directly as an Inner Parent to your Inner Child during your first three months. This especially includes trying to answer questions your Inner Child might ask during the session. Especially do not try to soothe your Inner Child because of an emotional answer it has given you. While some people think this is nurturing the Inner Child, it actually has the opposite effect. Respond only with, "Thank you, Inner Child, for telling me that." Sometimes you will ask your Inner Child a question and it will ask you a question back. If this happens, simply say, "Thank you, Inner Child, for telling me that," and then repeat the same question.

12. During sessions, you will often catch yourself responding automatically inside your mind as an Inner Parent. You will notice this is happening when your Inner Child is answering the question and you (as the Inner Parent) begin reacting to that answer. If you notice that you are doing this, stop, make a formal apology *OUT LOUD* and go back to the session's questions. Write out your apology in full on the left side of the paper as you speak it. Don't worry if you make frequent apologies. Awareness of this tendency is a big step in your growth. Your Inner Child will be im-pressed that you were aware of your automatic responses to its viewpoint

and that you apologized. Some practitioners have reported apologizing as many as 10 to 20 times during a session.

13. You may find yourself daydreaming as the Inner Parent during your session. When you catch yourself, simply apologize out loud in a similar manner as described above except substitute the word "daydreaming." This is also a normal experience for many practitioners during the beginning three months of Self-Parenting.

14. Each session should last 30 minutes—no more, no less. Even if you run out of time before you finish all the questions, just stop for that day and begin the next day with the next set of questions. If you finish all the questions early, continue your session by asking, "Inner Child, is there anything else you want to talk about?" If it says "No," then respond, "Thank you, Inner Child, for telling me that," and continue asking that question until the 30 minutes are up. *A VERY IMPORTANT PRINCIPLE OF THE SELF-PARENTING PROGRAM IS SPENDING A FULL HALF-HOUR WITH YOUR INNER CHILD.* You should not finish or quit early even at the Inner Child's suggestion. Spending this time is what communicates to your Inner Child that you care. Your Inner Child may test you in this regard by wanting to skip a session or quit early. If you stop the sessions early, you communicate that someone or something else is more important to you than your Inner Child. Extending your session past 30 minutes, even at your Inner Child's suggestion, is also a mistake.

15. After 30 minutes have passed, read the closing *OUT LOUD.* This officially ends your session.

Recommendations For After Your Sessions

16. Once you are finished with your session, don't try to practice impromptu sessions verbally or mentally during the day for the first three months. Let the effect of the session integrate into your life naturally. Trying to initiate dialogue about a "problem" during your first three months usually creates additional problems. Often this type of problem is created by the negative Inner Parent who is still being neglectful or abusive in some way.

Don't take the chance of exposing your Inner Child to potential abuse by rehashing issues outside your sessions.

17. A *definable* Inner Conflict is a different circumstance from the one described above. (See Inner Conflict section.) You are always better off resolving a true Inner Conflict as soon as you become aware of it. If you experience a true Inner Conflict outside your session, you must work it out as soon as possible. However, if you cannot define the conflict of needs, then you do not have an Inner Conflict. Review the Inner Conflict section to further understand the Inner Conflict procedures. After resolving 15 to 20 Inner Conflicts you will understand these steps much better.

18. Attend or organize a support group in your area. This is a guaranteed way to improve and develop your Self-Parenting style. Sharing your experiences with others can be very enlightening. A support group will also help to keep you faithful to your daily sessions.

19. Re-read the **SELF-PARENTING** book occasionally. There is a wealth of information within its pages and you will discover new ideas each time you read it. Review Parts I and II, as well as Part III.

20. Further your development with Self-Parenting Modules designed to deepen your experiences practicing the SELF-PARENTING Program. The suggested order is first the *Self-Esteem* and then the *Early Family & Childhood* modules. These will introduce you gently to the intermediate user levels of the SELF-PARENTING Program. There are also modules for advanced practitioners.

21. During your early days you may find it very helpful to meet with a therapist who understands the SELF-PARENTING Program. A professional can help you clarify difficult issues you may encounter due to your upbringing. Self-Parenting is simple, yet powerful. If the effects of your sessions aren't mostly positive, then you are doing something incorrectly or you need additional help.

22. Do not write out sessions with your opposite hand to "bring out the Inner Child." This technique adds unnecessary complexity to the ease of

the SELF-PARENTING Program. While this technique may have therapeutic value when used in other ways, within your Self-Parenting sessions it will be negative for the Inner Child. Also, we do not recommend using a tape recorder, typewriter or word processor to record your sessions.

23. Re-read Chapters 11 and 12 of **SELF-PARENTING.** It is amazing how many people either never read or don't remember reading these important chapters.

24. Once you complete the first two weeks of sessions from the book **SELF-PARENTING,** you must learn to make up your own questions. You may ask your Inner Child questions on any subject, but it is suggested you base your questions on your daily life. For example:

1. Inner Child, how are you doing this morning?
2. Inner Child, what would you like for breakfast?
3. Inner Child, what would you like to wear to work today?
4. Inner Child, what would you like to do Friday night?
5. Inner Child, how did you enjoy your weekend?
6. Inner Child, how do you feel about that upcoming job interview?
7. Inner Child, what should we do about _____ ?
8. Inner Child, what are your ideas about _____ ?
9. Inner Child, what do you recommend concerning _____ ?

Your questions should be open-ended and allow your Inner Child room to express itself.

25. Some Inner Parents believe that after they have spent only one month of sessions with their Inner Child they can ask deep, probing questions of the Inner Child regarding its neglect or abuse from family situations. This is a mistake. Remember, you are in the beginning stages of your relationship. You do not want to scare your Inner Child away. The need for "probing" is a mental need of the Inner Parent, not the Inner Child. It will take at least three months before your Inner Child can begin to trust you completely. Spend your time during the first three months "getting

to know" your Inner Child in a gentle, caring manner. You will be happier for it.

26. Always remember that whenever you ask a question, your only response will be, "Thank you, Inner Child, for telling me that." If you are unsure about making up your own questions, you may repeat the first two weeks of questions. It is quite normal to get different answers from your Inner Child. If you still have problems developing your own questions, take advantage of the modules from the SELF-PARENTING Program.

27. Keep in mind that if you have started sessions and then stopped them for a while, your Inner Child could be a bit unruly or hesitant about starting sessions again. This is because it feels betrayed already and starting sessions again could just lead to another betrayal. In this circumstance you must be ultra-careful that your Inner Parent does not miss or discontinue any sessions again.

28. Read each book recommended in Chapter Twelve of the book **SELF-PARENTING** to further your understanding of Self-Parenting. If you have read them before practicing half-hour sessions, then read them again. Once you have begun half-hour sessions, the information in these books will provide far greater insights for your Self-Parenting process than you experienced from reading them before practicing sessions. Be sure to relate them based on the dynamics between your Inner Parent and Inner Child, which will not relate necessarily to the way the book was intended originally by the author. Once you understand the dynamics of Self-Parenting, you can derive knowledge from many sources.

These procedures are vital to the success of your Self-Parenting. Changing them alters the basic structure of the SELF-PARENTING Program. Most people having problems with half-hour sessions of Self-Parenting have altered or omitted one or more of these steps. If someone tells you that they "know all about" Self-Parenting, compare what they say to these recommended procedures.

The SELF-PARENTING Program has created remarkable breakthroughs in the understanding of Self-Parenting, both in developing the process and creating the emotional/mental climate that enhances your growth. Every new practitioner should take full advantage of this fantastic tool. If you are currently a practitioner and you have been neglecting some of these procedures, change them and your sessions will improve dramatically.

YOUR RESPONSIBILITIES AS THE INNER PARENT

Being an Inner Parent entails a double responsibility. The first is to take care of your Inner Child and the second is to navigate a course for both selves in the outer world. The Inner Parent is responsible for conducting your half-hour sessions. Since the Inner Parent is "in charge" of the Self-Parenting relationship, it must take the leadership role in balancing the needs of the relationship. Leaving your life up to the Inner Child is like letting a child run a nursery school.

During the first three months of Self-Parenting, your Inner Parent must dedicate itself to a consistent practice of daily sessions to improve its Self-Parenting style. This will be particularly difficult for a disorganized or lazy Inner Parent, but you must make your best effort. You will have to provide a lot of "proof" that you have changed as an Inner Parent before your Inner Child will begin to trust you again. Your most important evidence will be consistent practice of your daily sessions.

Consistency with your daily session is crucial for success in Self-Parenting. If you are sporadic with your sessions, you will not get the cooperation you need from your Inner Child. If you are not consistent with your sessions, your Inner Child will simply refuse to respond. Your Inner Child is an important part of you that must be attended to every day. If you don't practice daily half-hour sessions, this means that someone or something is more important to you than your Inner Child.

For many people, the toughest part of Self-Parenting comes before actually sitting down to start the session. This is not because of the act of Self-Parenting itself, but because of the difficulty they have in arranging time to practice daily sessions. The Inner Parent seems to create many excuses and barriers before it is willing to get started. Some "don't like to write," others "know all about it," many can't be bothered.

A classic statement made by people who don't practice Self-Parenting and know they should is, "I don't have time to do sessions." What if an outer mother said to her family and friends, "I don't have time to pay attention to my child?" What would the legal authorities say if this mother completely abandoned her outer child? Who would respect the mother who spends all her time doing everything for everyone else's children but her own? And what could her neglected child do by itself during the day besides get into trouble? Amazingly, people do this exact same thing to their Inner Child. They abuse or neglect their Inner Child in this same manner without being aware of it.

You always find time to do what you feel is valuable. If you, as the Inner Parent, cannot find a half-hour a day to love, support and nurture your Inner Child, then your Inner Child is not valuable to you. If you have time to breathe, then you have time for your sessions. "I don't have time to do sessions" is Inner Child abuse, and it's time to stop abusing this most precious part of yourself.

Once you actually begin your sessions, however, you will feel great. The rush you get is fantastic, and each successive day gets easier and easier. But if your schedule is sporadic or infrequent, just sitting down to do a session becomes a chore. This is why it is so important to do your sessions every day, first thing in the morning. No time for resistance, no time for daily build-up; just get right to it and feel good right away. If you start your session quickly and easily, it's less time wasted. Begin this habit from your first day of Self-Parenting, and it will serve you well.

Purging

Practicing half-hour sessions has brought forth a curious phenomenon. When some people begin half-hour sessions, their Inner Child can use this opportunity to "purge" itself of frustrations that may have lain dormant for years. It seems that the Inner Child feels this might be the only chance it will have to be heard, and it wants to take this opportunity at any cost. Many people have experienced this phenomenon.

One person sitting down to do his exercises for the first time asked the Inner Child, "How are you today?" The first thing his Inner Child said was, "Where the HELL have you been all these years?" This was a strong sentiment for an Inner Child to express as its very first statement. Imagine if your father or mother had abandoned you long ago and then one day walked in the door and said, "Outer child, how are you today?" This is a similar experience occurring for many Self-Parenting practitioners.

Therefore, one certain result of your early Self-Parenting sessions will be to become more aware of the (usually unconscious) process you have of neglecting or abusing your Inner Child. For example, if your Inner Parent has been using denial as a safety valve, allowing your Inner Child to speak with acceptance is like opening the cap on an overheated radiator. For those first several minutes, there will be a lot of releasing steam.

In the beginning you may see much "steam" rising from your Inner Child. This is not a stated goal or purpose; it is just something that happens naturally during the early sessions. This is why it is so important for the Inner Parent to simply listen to what the Inner Child says, without judging or evaluating. Care and concern must be actively demonstrated by your Inner Parent through passively listening to your Inner Child. For many Inner Parents, these passive procedures take a great deal of willpower because their Inner Child may have been suppressed for years. It can be very difficult to listen to such abuse, accept it without commentary and respond by saying, "Thank you, Inner Child, for telling me that." Yet the results are well worth it.

A Special Caution

If you follow the prescribed half-hour format, it is impossible to offend your Inner Child *DURING* your session. It is possible, however, to run into trouble *OUTSIDE* your sessions if you try to "work with your Inner Child." Many new practitioners have had trouble with this. They are so excited to be doing sessions with their Inner Child that they want to continue dialoguing as an Inner Parent with their Inner Child outside their session. Because their sessions have gone so positively, they think that this "Inner Child work" is a snap. Unfortunately, what happens to these practitioners is that they become embroiled in a negative situation that escalates the more the Inner Parent presses the issue.

Your sessions go really smoothly because the format protects your Inner Child. All your Inner Parent is basically going to do is ask the Inner Child for some information or an opinion and say, "Thank you, Inner Child, for telling me that." Because the Inner Parent is using the session format, the Inner Child is safe and protected. Once you are out of the session, the negative Self-Parenting style of your Inner Parent surfaces. Because you now have a stronger, more in-tune Inner Child, it will be even quicker to resist the negative Inner Parent.

Yes, your Inner Parent wants to use the fantastic new awareness of Self-Parenting to finally "solve" the problem, but it is too soon. As an Inner Parent, you are still too negative outside your session. Attempting to "work with your Inner Child" during the day causes you to revert to your old (generally negative) Self-Parenting style, which only increases your stress. The more you attempt to resolve a Self-Parenting issue outside of your sessions, the more you will stir up the issue without resolving it. This is because positive Self-Parenting makes your Inner Child more conscious of and resistant to a negative Inner Parent.

When you are in your half-hour sessions, you are in them—and when you are out of them, you are out of them. After your session is over, just go back to your life. As the days and weeks pass, you will become more aware of the process of your Inner Conversations. You will certainly hear yourself talking to your Inner Child during the day. If you notice that you are being negative as an Inner Parent, then stop. You can even apologize as you do in your session. But don't try to "work with" your Inner Child during the day. This usually just makes the problem worse. This is especially true when it concerns a long-term issue such as food or smoking.

Just do your session, accept whatever comes up during that half-hour and then forget about it during the rest of your day. Continue to live your usual life, as an Inner Parent, until your next session. Outside your sessions let your Inner Child say whatever it wants, negative, positive or indifferent. At most, you can respond to your Inner Child with "Thank you, Inner Child, for telling me that," and let the rest go until the next day's session.

Issues Of The Past

Many new practitioners want to explore issues of the past. They want to dig deeply into their psycho-sexual-family history to uncover their worst childhood traumas, hoping this will solve their current problems. But what you really need to do right now is to solve your current life problems by working through current solutions. The reason for your unhappiness right now is the quality of your Self-Parenting interaction today. If you have a problem today, solve that problem today. The key to solving present problems is to become conscious of what you are currently thinking and feeling and base your actions on meeting your current needs.

Even if unconscious childhood traumas are contributing to your present unhappiness, resolving your current issues is the key to clearing up the past. The problems you have today are the result of Self-Parenting decisions you made yesterday. Your experience of tomorrow will be created by the Self-Parenting decisions you make today. The more positive and supportive your Self-Parenting style right now, the brighter your future will be.

Your beginning months of Self-Parenting are not the time to work on your deepest and most painful issues. Dredging up negative experiences from your past is not very helpful either. Your early Self-Parenting sessions are designed for you, as the Inner Parent, to establish a new relationship with your Inner Child—someone you lost touch with long ago.

The SELF-PARENTING Program provides a developmentally appropriate practice for the process of learning positive Self-Parenting skills. And yet, learning positive Self-Parenting skills isn't easy; it's a whole new process. You have never done this before, and you don't yet have any real training.

Your first step as the Inner Parent is simply to listen to your Inner Child—not to change it, but to become more conscious of this inner voice. Later, as you become more aware of what you are thinking and feeling, you can change any negatives to positives. These procedures and guidelines have been developed over a 20-year period and include the experience of thousands of practitioners. Following these procedures will assure your happiness and success before moving on to the next level of challenge.

WHY SESSIONS ARE A HALF-HOUR

Some authorities on the Inner Child have stated that you don't need to spend more than a few minutes a day with your Inner Child. The SELF-PARENTING Program disagrees with these statements. As a practitioner of the SELF-PARENTING Program, you must spend 30 minutes a day, on an ongoing basis to receive the long-term benefits for which you are searching.

Self-Parenting sessions aren't necessarily all fun and games. Your sessions will be like life itself, sometimes dull, sometimes exciting, but always moving forward. Your Inner Child may be subject to intense emotional releases, or your sessions could be boring and flat. Sometimes you will feel as if it takes an hour to do one half-hour session. Sometimes you will think only minutes have gone by before the clock says your session is over. Although your subjective experience of time may vary, it is important to keep your session to 30 minutes, not less or more, because of the effect it has on your Inner Child.

Your Inner Child's reality is governed by the time on the clock, not the subjective experience of your session. For example, your Inner Child may complain at some point during your session that it doesn't want to do the session. It may kick and scream for 15 minutes about wanting to stop or being bored. You may be tempted as the Inner Parent to quit early to "nurture" your Inner Child by giving in to it. Instead, continue writing down everything your Inner Child says and repeating, "Thank You, Inner Child, for telling me that," until your time is up.

How will your Inner Child react once your session is over? You will probably find an amazing rush of warmth and happiness from your Inner Child. Why? Because it is extremely relieved and gratified that you continued your session, even though it complained about wanting to stop. If you had stopped the session early because of what the Inner Child was saying, your Inner Child would have resented the fact that it didn't get its full 30 minutes.

During one session I personally listened to my Inner Child complain for 25 full and long minutes that it didn't want to do our session. Finally, I said, "Okay, we'll end this session early just for you," and quit. The first words from my Inner Child the next morning were, "Why did you stop our session five minutes early yesterday?" My response? "Thank you, Inner Child, for telling me that."

Let's look at half-hour sessions from another perspective. Imagine you were a parent spending 30 minutes each day with your outer child. He or she would be grateful to enjoy your complete attention for that amount of time. At the same time, depending on its mood or energy each day, your child might want to postpone or cancel your session. But since you have established a consistent pattern and are sticking to it, your child will derive self-esteem from your half-hour of attention each day. Years later your child would probably remember little of what was said or done during specific sessions, but he or she will always remember and appreciate the fact that you shared your time together.

You are establishing this same type of program as an Inner Parent for your Inner Child. Regardless of the day-to-day content of your session, the overriding benefit is that your Inner Child discovers and experiences that it will be loved, supported and nurtured for 30 minutes each day. The positive effects of practicing half-hour sessions go far beyond what happens in any given session.

Someone might ask, "Can I do 10 minutes three times a day instead of 30 minutes all at once?" or "Why can't I go longer if I want to?" Thirty minutes is the ideal time to spend each day with your Inner Child. It is the amount of time from which you will receive the greatest benefit with the least effort. Ten minutes or less is not enough time to do anything. It takes two minutes just to say the opening and write down the time and date. And trying to do anything regularly three times a day in a busy schedule is almost impossible.

Thirty minutes is also an easy amount of clock time to record as opposed to say, 22 minutes or 35 minutes. You will find it very easy to "chunk" time into a half-hour segment. Thirty minutes is especially convenient for those who follow a schedule. You will know, for example, that every morning from 6:00 to 6:30 a.m. you and your Inner Child are going to be together.

Thirty minutes is also enough time and yet not so much time that you can't find a half-hour to devote to your Inner Child. No matter how busy you think you are, if you can't find 30 minutes in your day to spend with your Inner Child, you **NEED** to take a half-hour and spend it with your Inner Child. Most practitioners say that from each half-hour they spend with their Inner Child, they gain an extra two hours of time and energy during the day. In other words, if you can't "find" a half-hour, your negative Inner Parent is preventing you from accessing an extra two hours a day.

Spending 30 minutes **EVERY DAY** with your Inner Child also has an important psychological factor. Thirty minutes is a definable slot in your day. As you begin spending this substantial amount of time with your Inner Child, it begins to feel important. It knows that 30 minutes is significant in the life of a busy Inner Parent, so it respects you for being willing to take this time.

Thirty minutes is also enough time for both Inner Selves to explore a major issue or complaint in depth. You will soon realize that 10 or 20 minutes feel like 10 or 20 seconds when you have a substantial issue to discuss. You might even say to your Inner Child if it hems or haws, "Look, Inner Child, we have only 30 minutes. If you want to say something, you'd better get moving or you'll miss out." This way your Inner Child knows that it can't afford to dawdle or waste time or it won't get its needs met. Thirty minutes leaves enough time to discuss and resolve most situations that come up.

If 30 minutes is so good, why not go for an hour? Well, that would be great. On the other hand, an hour is major time for the busy person in today's world. Even if you had an hour to devote to your Inner Child occasionally, you may not always have that option. A big key to the success of the session is that it is for a set time. If you spend an extended amount of time with your Inner Child because you are on vacation for a few weeks and then cut back down to 30 minutes, your Inner Child will feel deprived. It is much safer to stick to a time you can always commit to and leave it at that.

Some people say that their early sessions during the first two weeks don't last 30 minutes. Usually they are not writing down the questions properly or they are skipping some of the procedures in some way. Perhaps their Inner Child is giving only one-word answers because it doesn't quite believe what is happening.

Stick to the full amount of time for your sessions right from the beginning. This is what demonstrates to your Inner Child by actions, not words, that you are going to "be there" for it. Your Inner Child should be able to count on spending 30 minutes by the clock. If you do 25 minutes here and 28 there, your Inner Child will know that you are cheating and it will hold back much more than two or five minutes worth of time from your sessions. Why? Because it knows that you still can't be trusted as an Inner Parent.

Thirty minutes each day devoted to your Inner Child provides a reasonable, substantial and stable platform from which you, as the Inner Parent, can develop a positive Self-Parenting style. The SELF-PARENTING Program has tested this time period over a multitude of situations and life-styles. Stick with it and you can't go wrong.

3

YOUR FIRST THREE MONTHS

The Problem

Your first three months of Self-Parenting are the most illuminating of your life. Because you are learning a new skill AND experiencing powerful emotions, you may find yourself on a rollercoaster ride. Depending on the type of outer parenting you received, you could encounter different types of problems.

The Solution

Be consistent with your daily practice of the SELF-PARENTING Program. Become familiar with the types of problems that a new practitioner may have. Read this section many times to prepare and educate your Inner Parent. Join a support group and/or work with a therapist who practices Self-Parenting so you can share your experiences with other practitioners.

GUIDELINES FOR THE FIRST THREE MONTHS

During your first three months of practicing half-hour sessions, you should spend the majority of your time, as the Inner Parent, just asking questions and listening to your Inner Child's answers. Although it may seem passive, it takes a very strong Inner Parent to follow this advice. Your main challenge is to remain positive and avoid the negative patterns learned from your outer parenting, a tricky task for most Inner Parents.

It is not easy just to listen. In fact, for the average Inner Parent, simply listening is quite difficult. After all, how often did your parents ask you a question and then allow you to respond exactly the way you wanted to, for as long as you wanted, without any negative feedback?

If you had mostly negative role models as a child, you will have developed mostly negative Self-Parenting skills. Therefore, the first skills you must develop during your first three months of sessions are:

- Ask questions only
- Listen carefully to the answers and record them completely
- Thank your Inner Child for giving you its answers
- Resist any impulses to evaluate, change or comment on your Inner Child's answers

Thankfully, the session format will do just that. Also, by asking questions of your Inner Child, you will learn more than you ever thought possible.

Many times your questions will evoke a strong emotional response from your Inner Child. Trying to soothe, advise or comfort your emotional Inner Child during your early sessions is actually negative Self-Parenting. Your only response to the hurt or hostile emotions of your Inner Child should be, "Thank you, Inner Child, for telling me that." This is by far the most effective approach. Not only is this the safest way to prevent yourself from becoming a negative Inner Parent, it is also the first time in its life that your Inner Child will have been heard completely without negative feedback.

During your first three months of Self-Parenting, three enhancements occur simultaneously in the relationship between your Inner Parent and Inner Child. You are:

1. Building trust
2. Establishing consistency
3. Creating the awareness to open communication between your Inner Parent and Inner Child

Building Trust

Prior to starting half-hour sessions, your Inner Child knew that you, as the Inner Parent, were not listening to it. This caused your Inner Child to feel isolated and unloved, which resulted in your Inner Child not trusting you. How would you feel if every time you went to your parents to share your experience or express your concerns, you were neglected or abused instead?

Unfortunately, most people do not care enough about their Inner Child to grant it a daily half-hour of attention. This proves to the Inner Child that it is not important to the Inner Parent, i.e., that it is unloved. Attention equals love as far as your Inner Child is concerned. If you always promise your best friend you are going to get together but you never make the time, what does that tell your best friend? What does that say about you as a friend? In a similar manner, many people pay only lip service to or completely ignore their Inner Child. Conducting daily half-hour sessions as the Inner Parent puts you in an elite group of people actually practicing what they preach.

Daily sessions of Self-Parenting also show your Inner Child that you are committed to caring for it on a physical, "real world" basis. Thirty minutes of your precious time represents a serious commitment that your Inner Child knows it must appreciate. Even though you may have established a new high in your Self-Parenting relationship by starting sessions, your Inner Child is not sure you will continue. Only after a period of about three months will your Inner Child, begrudgingly perhaps, become convinced enough to trust that you will continue giving it the attention it so desperately craves.

Establishing Consistency

Consistency is very important to your Inner Child. Consistency over time is the proof your Inner Child requires before it believes you will continue sessions. After all, you have started positive programs before and then quit them. Consistency with your sessions guarantees your Inner Child that it will have the time needed to talk and share with you on a daily basis. It also gives you the time to work out problems you may have with each other.

Ninety days is the approximate amount of time it takes for the average Inner Child to develop a stable foundation of trust and security and to feel confident that the Inner Parent will continue these precious sessions as part of its daily routine.

Creating Awareness to Open Communication

Before starting half-hour sessions, your perception of which voice is your Inner Parent and which is your Inner Child is unclear. Each session during your first three months contributes to more certainty and understanding in this regard. If you are in a support group, you will probably have at least two or three episodes during the first three months in which you discover the voice you thought was your Inner Child was actually your Inner Parent or vice versa. For example, one Self-Parenting student was flabbergasted when it was pointed out by his support group members that it was his Inner Child who wanted to clean the car on Saturday morning, not his Inner Parent.

You will also find many occasions during the first three months in which the voice of your Inner Child will surprise you by popping up during the day. Or you may become aware of negative emotions or body stress just as you realize your Inner Parent is neglecting or abusing your Inner Child. These insights during the early months of Self-Parenting are important signs of your progress. They will continue throughout your first year of sessions.

It is important to keep in mind that you cannot buy respect from your Inner Child. Respect from your Inner Child comes automatically when you, as the Inner Parent, do the following things:

1. Be honest with your Inner Child
2. Spend consistent time paying attention to the needs of your Inner Child
3. Make a sincere effort to create the best choices possible for both Inner Selves

By faithfully following the session guidelines you will be well rewarded. No matter what your Inner Child says, if you, as the Inner Parent, can lovingly respond with, "Thank you, Inner Child, for telling me that," then you have proven you know how to listen. Ideally, sometime during the first three months, your Inner Child will finally sense that its feelings or suggestions are now being heard and accepted, not abused or ignored, by the Inner Parent.

The Many Moods of Your Inner Child

Some psychological systems of analyzing your Inner Conversations describe as many as 30 or 40 inner voices. They give a different name to each voice and try to differentiate the "inner critic" from the "angry warrior" or the "hurt inner child" from the "angry inner child." Other systems say there can be several types of Inner Parents, the "inner mother," the "grand taskmaster," or the "inner uncle-in-law." These systems differ in philosophy, terminology and the number of voices to identify.

The SELF-PARENTING Program teaches that only two voices make up your Inner Conversations — the Inner Parent and Inner Child. But *EACH INNER*

SELF CAN EXPRESS DIFFERENT MOODS. This explains the discrepancy. You only have one Inner Parent voice, but depending on the way it feels at any particular moment, it could seem like many different personalities. Just like an outer child, your Inner Child can feel any emotion under the sun at any time and reverse emotions at any minute. This does not make it a different voice or personality, however.

Self-Parenting practitioners quickly find out when they begin writing down their Inner Conversations on paper (rather than speaking them out loud to a therapist), that they only have two voices. As they learn to identify these two (and only two) personalities, they learn to distinguish the different moods and perspectives of each Inner Self. This advanced technical knowledge of the Inner Conversations is one reason why the SELF-PARENTING Program is so effective.

The Age of Your Inner Child

One Self-Parenting student said, "My sessions aren't working because my five-year-old doesn't feel like she's five." The question is, "Who told this person that her Inner Child had to be five years old?"

Your Inner Child's personality can express any age, from one minute old to age 20. On certain days it may act three years old, on other days it may act 15. There is no way to set a specific age for the Inner Child. This is also why we do not differentiate between an "inner adolescent" and the Inner Child. The positive Inner Parent uses Self-Parenting methods appropriate for any age Inner Child, while remaining alert to the possibility of changes as the Inner Child matures or regresses in age.

If you, as an outer parent, have a child who is six months old, you must provide a completely different support system than if the child is 8 or 15 years old. Similarly, your Inner Child will need much more teaching and support when it is behaving at a younger age. As your Inner Child expresses a stronger and more independent self, you will need to grant your Inner Child more independence and autonomy as an Inner Parent.

How do you tell what age your Inner Child is expressing at the moment? By the information and the manner in which your Inner Child responds to you. Using the methods of the SELF-PARENTING Program, you easily adapt to the various ages of your Inner Child without realizing it. In this way the SELF-PARENTING Program handles situations in a positive manner that you may not even be aware of consciously.

As your sessions accumulate, you will begin noticing your Inner Child's viewpoint more often outside your sessions. As you become more attuned to your Inner Conversations, you will become conscious of your negative Self-Parenting. You will begin to notice the protests from your Inner Child when it reacts to abuse or neglect. Begin to use these opportunities outside your session to tune in to your Inner Child as it expresses its needs.

In general, don't concern yourself with the age of your Inner Child or whether having a younger or older Inner Child is better. All the techniques associated with the SELF-PARENTING Program are designed to be helpful whatever the "age" of your Inner Child. The truth is that your Inner Child is changing attitudes and perspectives on a daily basis anyway; you are going to work hard just keeping up the pace. More importantly, your Inner Child will continue to grow and mature as your practice of Self-Parenting continues. What you have to worry about is your Inner Parent learning and keeping up with the pace of your Inner Child.

Yes! The Inner Child Can Sound Like the Inner Parent

A frequent comment heard from those in the early stages of the SELF-PARENTING Program is, "My Inner Child keeps telling me what to do," or "My Inner Child sounds like the Inner Parent!" Usually this experience is unsettling to the new practitioner and often confuses the Inner Parent, who begins to wonder if the Inner Child's voice is really the Inner Parent or "What exactly is happening?"

Don't worry if this happens to you. To have your Inner Child sound like an Inner Parent is very normal and predictable during the first few months of practice. After an explanation, you will easily understand this phenomenon and learn how to deal with it in the prescribed Self-Parenting manner.

There are three types of situations in which your Inner Child "sounds like an Inner Parent." In the first situation, you notice your Inner Child keeps telling you what you (as the Inner Parent) have done wrong, are doing wrong or will do wrong, thus sounding "like an Inner Parent."

During your Self-Parenting sessions, your Inner Child gets to speak — and boy, does it use this opportunity at times! The things it comes up with are often directly to the point, accusatory or very uncomfortable for the Inner Parent to bear.

"You forgot _____."
"Why didn't you _____?"
"You promised _____ and then you _____."
"You lied when you _____."

You should be listening carefully. These statements often point out the exact flaws that you, as an Inner Parent, continue to manifest unconsciously as a part of your deeper Self-Parenting style. Now, since you are giving it the opportunity, your Inner Child is only too happy to point out your negative actions and behaviors. Since you are asking your Inner Child's opinion, it will be more than happy to give it to you!

If your Inner Child is complaining about some aspect of you, as an Inner Parent, it is probably correct. Since this is an analysis, these comments can sound like the Inner Parent or even like a therapist. In reality, they are your Inner Child's accurate observations. Pay attention and resolve to change any negative Self-Parenting behaviors that your Inner Child points out. This is one reason why you are practicing half-hour sessions in the first place.

Practitioners are often surprised by how intelligent and aware their Inner Child can be. Just because we are calling this voice the Inner Child doesn't mean it is not smart. Practitioners often comment on how insightfully the Inner Child can analyze a problem and come up with a solution. After all, your Inner Child has been absorbing knowledge for as long as you have. Because the Inner Child is the intuitive self and has a holistic point of view, it can easily have more insight on a situation than you, as the "rational" Inner

Parent. In the second situation you will hear criticisms made by your Inner Child that are extremely negative or critical, above and beyond reality. In this situation you may be getting in touch with some of your Inner Child's buried hostility and resentment. If your Inner Child has deeply suppressed emotions such as anger, guilt or fear, your Self-Parenting sessions will bring these deeper feelings to the surface so they can be released.

Do not be dismayed if you experience strong or emotional outbursts from your Inner Child right off the bat. Unfortunately, if emotional outbursts were part of your childhood, this may be what comes up in your early sessions. The good news is that just on the other side of this buried negativity is a wellspring of positive emotions that will flood you just as strongly in a positive way.

Whether the emotions of your Inner Child are positive or negative, the SELF-PARENTING Program works the same way. Whatever comments your Inner Child makes, write them down exactly and say out loud, "Thank you, Inner Child, for telling me that." This way your Inner Child is heard and acknowledged without any negative feedback or abuse from the Inner Parent.

Another possible cause of strong negativity or resistance comes from not realizing how tricky your Inner Child can be. The Inner Child often tries to test you to see if you really are going to listen and accept whatever it says. It is smart enough to test you in a way that is guaranteed to strike at your weakest point. It wants to find out right away if you are going to stick with the program or not. Therefore it might say exactly what it knows you don't want to hear, just to see if you are strong enough to follow the format.

To explore a third reason why an Inner Child might make statements that "sound like an Inner Parent," ask yourself the following question, "Where did my Inner Child learn to behave?" The answer, of course, is from your outer parents or caretakers. So if what comes out of your Inner Child's mouth sounds "Inner Parental," then guess what? It is! Your Inner Child is simply speaking back to you in the way it was taught to speak. If, instead of being allowed to be a child, it was constantly pressured to "grow up" and be a "young lady" or a "young man," then this is what it is attempting to do.

The beauty of the SELF-PARENTING Program is that whether your Inner Child is:

Pointing out your flaws . . .
Releasing . . .
Or simply acting like an Inner Parent . . .

the process is the same. First you ask a question, next you write down exactly what your Inner Child says, then you say, "Thank you, Inner Child, for telling me that." After your session is over, go back to your life and enjoy it the best way you know how.

When the Inner Child Is the Motivator

Most people don't realize how much socialization is necessary for the human infant to achieve even minimal standards of functionality. Children only learn what their significant others teach them. Our self-image is created by the way we are treated in our early years by adults. If we learn as children that no one will be there for us, then we cannot be there for ourselves. Without positive role models to emulate, we will have no internal experience upon which to base positive behavior.

During a child's early family life, the positive parent will pay attention and respond appropriately to the outer child. A major aspect of the parent's role is to motivate the outer child to be successful and to achieve. By receiving positive motivation and encouragement from the behavior of its parents, the child will grow to be motivated and achievement-oriented as an adult.

Surprisingly, when some people begin practicing the Self-Parenting Program, they find that their Inner Child is the one motivating their Inner Parent. In fact, for many beginning practitioners, their Inner Child is much more in touch with reality than their Inner Parent. Although this seems great on the surface, it still represents a negative condition in their Self-Parenting style. First of all, the Inner Child is carrying responsibility that is actually the role of the Inner Parent. Secondly, it causes the already weak Inner Parent to become even more confused and helpless.

An outer child should be able to experience being a child. It is role-dependent on the parent for guidance during times of trouble or stress. When there is a problem, the child should be able to say, "Hey, I'm scared, I need your help. Because I trust you, I know you will guide me and take care of me." Ideally, the outer parent is responsible and skillful enough to support and nurture the child in this manner.

However, with dysfunctional outer parenting, as in the case of alcoholic parents, the outer child is often forced to assume the parental, caretaker role. Because the parents are unable to function, the child is the one cleaning the house, making the meals and paying the bills. Even though such a child is seen as "responsible" and "mature" by outsiders, he or she is still a child inside. Unfortunately, this type of pressure and responsibility typically becomes part of the Inner Child's personality. In this type of circumstance, the Inner Child is going to be stronger than its Inner Parent because the outer parents were weaker than it was as a child. This creates the condition of the Inner Child sounding like your Inner Parent.

Another cause of the Inner Child leading the Inner Parent occurs when the outer parents haven't listened, acknowledged or supported the child when it was young. Since the outer parents weren't strong enough or confident enough to support the child, only through the Inner Child's desire and initiative did anything get accomplished. In this situation the Inner Child is again forced to assert itself and to aggressively stake out its own achievements.

This role reversal explains why your Inner Child can be stronger in many ways than your Inner Parent, but what can you do? For many people beginning the SELF-PARENTING Program, their Inner Parent is incapable of positive Self-Parenting at first. This is another reason why the format is so structured. In your early sessions, just be sure to always respond to your Inner Child's statements with, "Thank you, Inner Child, for telling me that." This always protects the Inner Child and gives you practice becoming more supportive as a listener. As you progress in Self-Parenting, you will find that the two Inner Selves will gradually assume their more traditional roles. The ultra-responsible Inner Child will become more childlike, and the weak and ineffectual Inner Parent will become more responsible and directive.

Achieving Success

Success is enjoying your life. True success in the outer world is based on your success within the inner world of your Inner Conversations. Outer success means nothing if it is not accompanied by the happiness and fulfillment that comes from positive Self-Parenting. You may be rich, powerful, successful and have every external trapping of success. But if your Inner Parent practices a negative Self-Parenting style, your Inner Child will never be truly happy.

Once your Self-Parenting style is positive, achieving success in the outer world is a goal worth having. Directing yourself toward success in the outer world is the job of your Inner Parent, yet many of you are failing. One question to answer in this regard is, "How many things have you wanted to do for a long time that you haven't done?" If you made a list right now, would you have many items on this list? For some of you it would be quite a few.

True success in the outer world is doing what you want to do in life. If you have goals or dreams that are dormant or dead, then your life is dormant or dead. You are just going through the motions like a robot following someone else's command. If you want outer success, you will have to earn it the old-fashioned way, by working hard for it. If you want success on the inside, you will also have to earn it, through half-hour sessions with your Inner Child.

If you have only enough energy for the pursuit of one form of happiness, concentrate on the inner world. Once you are happy on the inside, you will find it makes the outer world more livable. Then you can go for outer success. If you spend all your time seeking the outer world's version of happiness, you may find yourself chasing a rainbow that doesn't exist. Or once you arrive, you will still find yourself unhappy because your Self-Parenting style hasn't changed.

Being obsessed about or trying to change or control the behavior of your Inner Child is not going to make you happy. Your most direct path to happiness is to create a positive Inner Parent who will meet the needs of your Inner Child and whose own needs are being met in the process.

Outer Parenting

Outer parenting has come a long way since the early 1900s. A popular child care book of the 1920s gave advice such as, "Never hug your child and never let them sit on your lap." Even as late as the 1950s mothers were told to let their babies cry in their cribs so as not to let them become "spoiled" by having mother at their beck and call.

The "experts" said that if children were constantly attended to when young, they would become spoiled and unable to cope with the reality of the "real world." Instead, of course, this style of parenting created emotionally crippled children by denying them the foundation of love and security they needed to function in society. As a result, this advice created the exact situation it was supposed to prevent.

Today, of course, we know this style of parenting to be incorrect. The comfort, safety and security experienced from constant nurture and support are what allow a child to internalize its strength of personality. Without this internal experience of being loved, cared for, and nurtured, it is next to impossible to feel psychologically secure as an adult.

Self-Esteem and Happiness

Happiness for us humans is not just a matter of food, water and a roof over our heads. Happiness, a positive and healthy sense of self-esteem, is something we learn. When you were conceived, you received a brand new nervous system. Every experience you had was neurologically recorded for future use. Your first opportunity to experience happiness and self-esteem was from your parents. If you weren't given this experience by your parents, then it will be difficult for you to learn it elsewhere.

Some practitioners already have a strong sense of self-esteem. They were the fortunate ones who had love, support and nurturing from their parents when growing up. They are basically happy with their lives most of the time. When they experience temporary setbacks or personal misfortune, they can usually bounce back with help from a friend, a change of environment or time to grieve.

Others do not have as much self-esteem. For them, happiness is a temporary state that comes and goes depending upon external circumstances. If things happen to go their way, they will enjoy high self-esteem. If things don't go their way, they have low self-esteem.

Even if you missed your opportunity to experience happiness and self-esteem as a child, you can learn to give this to yourself as an adult. The surest way to achieve self-esteem is to establish a positive relationship of loving, supporting and nurturing interactions between your Inner Parent and Inner Child. Working consciously with your Inner Child creates this positive sense of self-esteem and internal happiness.

Improving Outer Relationships

Positive outer relationships are a major priority on everyone's wish list. Yet the most important relationship of all, that between your Inner Parent and your Inner Child, is largely mishandled or ignored. This is doubly negative since the key to enjoying positive relationships with others is to first establish this type of relationship with your Inner Child. As you improve the Self-Parenting relationship between your Inner Parent and Inner Child, you will find all your other relationships improving to an equal degree.

THE FOUNDATION OF YOUR RELATIONSHIPS WITH OTHERS IS THE QUALITY OF THE RELATIONSHIP YOU HAVE WITH YOURSELF.

As you develop advanced communication skills within your Inner Conversations, you will automatically transfer these skills to your outer relationships. Loving, supporting and nurturing your Inner Child will give you the foundation from which to love, support and nurture others. In fact, your outer relationships are the direct reflection or mirror of your Self-Parenting relationship.

A common observation among practitioners who begin Self-Parenting is that they often let go of at least two or three dysfunctional outer relationships almost immediately. Because they begin fulfilling their needs directly, they don't need to be in a relationship that fulfills certain needs but also brings disadvantages. You too may find that if you are in a negative or toxic relationship, you will just let go of that relationship. In most cases this is not a conscious decision with an agonizing withdrawal. You simply do it and notice that you have ended the relationship after the fact.

Here is an interesting question you might ask yourself concerning your outer relationships:

> If you treated your friends the same way you treat yourself, would you have any friends?

Another big advantage of practicing the SELF-PARENTING Program is that your half-hour sessions teach primary communication skills to both Inner Selves. Without even realizing it, you will automatically apply these skills to your outer relationships — at no extra charge!

Link to the Past and Future

Your future growth in Self-Parenting involves strengthening and maintaining the relationship you have with your Inner Child. This requires an active role by the Inner Parent and is a complicated area to master. The difficulty is to remain positive and not slip back into any negative patterns held over from your upbringing.

But remember, you cannot speed your growth in Self-Parenting by "doing more faster." Your Inner Child lives in the "real world." It wants to see some calendar time go by before it fully believes that you, as the Inner Parent, are going to be consistent with your sessions. It may hope, it may pray, it may even resist kicking and screaming, but until you, as the Inner Parent, have spent 100 or more half-hour sessions with your Inner Child, it will not become a believer.

As you continue practicing sessions, your Inner Child will sound less and less like an Inner Parent. As you access deeper levels of your Self-Parenting style, your Inner Child will become more childlike. As your sessions continue, both selves will naturally settle into more traditional-sounding roles regardless of where you started. In six months your sessions will be completely different from the ones you are having now.

Each of us is connected within the continuum of time to our past and our future. Our link with the past is through our parents; our connection to the future is via our children. Self-Parenting practitioners are fully immersed in the key link between their past and future — their Self-Parenting style. They know that these factors have been internalized as the Inner Parent and the Inner Child. As the first person in your continuum to practice conscious Self-Parenting, you carry a responsibility far beyond your own individual life. You may be the first person in your family line to stop the transmission of dysfunctional and negative Self-Parenting traits to future generations.

SELF-PARENTING SUPPORT GROUPS

The most effective route to a positive Self-Parenting style is to start or join a SELF-PARENTING Support Group for at least three to six months. This is the approximate amount of time you will need to fully integrate the practical principles of Self-Parenting into the "real world." Social interaction has a profound impact on learning. This is why we encourage you to work with a group to help strengthen your Inner Parent. Remember, technically speaking, Self-Parenting is "Inner Parent work," not Inner Child work, and your Inner Parent needs all the outside help it can get.

You will find the support of other practitioners a big help during your early months of sessions. Self-Parenting appears to be a simple enough process. One sits down, follows the session protocol for 30 minutes and that's it. It appears to be easy to do even without someone there to guide you. All you have to do is do sessions every day, feel fantastic and life gets better and better. Right?

Well, all of the above can be true. But the average new practitioner needs encouragement. Most people have difficulty sticking with their sessions once the first two weeks of questions are up. Daily sessions of Self-Parenting can be difficult to sustain without an external support system. It is not so much the pressures of the outside world as the weakness of the Inner Parent.

And make no mistake about it — not doing daily sessions is the fault of a weak Inner Parent. Whatever the excuses or denials, it is the uncaring or negative Inner Parent who will not set aside 30 minutes for the most important person in his or her life, the Inner Child.

Support Groups Love, Support and Nurture Your Growth

Before it can grow, a young seedling may need support, perhaps extra watering, protection from the wind or a carefully-placed stake for guidance. Once it takes root, it is capable of surviving on its own under normal conditions.

Many people who begin conscious Self-Parenting do not do so under normal conditions. In fact, they may have never experienced "normal" at all. When you begin Self-Parenting, a significant amount of emotional life is being born, which could be susceptible to early damage if not cared for correctly.

Changing the Self-Parenting procedures, even inadvertently, can be like forgetting to water a plant for a few days or having the stake fall out of the ground. Hardy plants will survive, but weaker ones won't. A support group can help keep you keep on the path during your first few months of Self-Parenting. Take advantage of the opportunity to start or join a support group if at all possible. Groups can be as individual as the people in them, and several successful group formats have evolved. The important thing is to stick with the group and add your positive energy. Most ongoing groups consist of six to eight people who get together every week. They often close the meeting once they have their core people, and members don't seem to drop out. Another option is to follow the SELF-PARENTING Program one-month support group guidelines, and then have an advanced group for those who have gone through the four-week format a few times.

All members of the group should be practicing Self-Parenting sessions. If they are not, they will not grow with the other members of the group. Although members can provide each other encouragement, each person must ultimately make the personal commitment for daily sessions with his or her Inner Child. People who don't practice half-hour sessions, yet attend a group just so they can "talk about" their Inner Child, siphon off the positive energy the group is creating.

Attending a meeting one night a week will help all members get the most benefit out of their daily sessions. It is amazing how much meeting with other practitioners for a two-hour session once a week can help one's individual practice.

If you compare learning to Self-Parent with learning how to swim, your first month of Self-Parenting is like sprinkling yourself with a hose on a hot day. It will take the average person at least three months of daily practice to begin to understand the process. Learning to swim means that you are able to swim, dive or hold your breath underwater. One-month practitioners often build a sense of false security which doesn't stand the test of time. They know a little bit about themselves and the Self-Parenting process, but they have only begun to get their feet wet.

How to Start/Conduct a SELF-PARENTING® Support Group

If there is no registered group in your area, here are some guidelines for starting your own meeting. Many practitioners of Self-Parenting are already familiar with one of the many types of support group formats such as ACA, OA, NA or AA. These programs are based on the 12-Step philosophy.

The SELF-PARENTING Support Groups, however, follow a different format for a new purpose — to provide a support system for people practicing daily sessions of positive Self-Parenting with their Inner Child. Many groups begin with friends who have read and benefited from *SELF-PARENTING: The Complete Guide to Your Inner Conversations.* They meet simply to share their insights. Early meetings have consisted of as few as three or four people.

A SELF-PARENTING Support Group can be easily formed by any group of committed participants. "Committed" in this case means that each group member is willing to meet for the minimum of four sessions and that each person is willing to practice the half-hour sessions each day with their Inner Child. This commitment will build trust and intimacy within the group.

Each meeting is based on a simple four-week format of sharing, reading, questions and homework. In the intimate environment of a support group, this format can be a very effective introduction to the practice of positive Self-Parenting.

Incidentally, newcomers should only be admitted at the first meeting each month. This is to protect the practicing support group members during the second, third, or fourth meetings. Newcomer doubts and lack of commitment have been found to take away from the growth and sharing experienced by the group once they have begun daily sessions together.

Meeting One

Sharing: The first meeting of the month serves as a "getting to know you" and "introduction to Self-Parenting" session for participants. Members introduce themselves and give some background on their personal journeys. The format for the next three weeks is discussed and any questions are answered. Each member should have a copy of the book **SELF-PARENTING** by this time and have read through at least Chapter Eight before the meeting.

Reading: Group members read Chapter Nine of **SELF-PARENTING** out loud.

Questions: Any questions about session procedures based on the reading are asked and discussed.

Homework: Each person makes a personal commitment to his or her Inner Child and the group. Everyone begins practicing the daily sessions of Self-Parenting the very next morning using the questions from Week One.

Meeting Two

Sharing: Each member shares his or her experience of practicing the first week of sessions. When a group of people assemble to discuss their Self-Parenting progress, it is usually easy to share experiences. To find that another person's thoughts, feelings and experiences with Self-Parenting are so similar to your own is amazing. Plenty of time is available for sharing during this second meeting.

Reading: Group members read Chapter Ten of **SELF-PARENTING** out loud (this is a very short reading). If there have been many problems during the week, it may be helpful to review or reread Chapter Nine.

Questions: Any questions are asked and discussed.

Homework: Each person does the sessions from Week Two each morning.

Meeting Three

Sharing: Each member shares his or her experience with the questions from the second week.

Reading: Group members read Chapter 11 out loud.

Questions: Any questions based on the reading are discussed.

Homework: The third week of sessions consists of group members creating their own questions for the sessions each morning. This next week represents a big step in the practice of positive Self-Parenting.

Meeting Four

Sharing: Group members share their experiences designing their own sessions as the Inner Parent.

Reading: Group members read Chapter 12 out loud.

Questions: Questions based on the reading are asked and discussed.

Homework: Each committed member now has a beginning knowledge of the SELF-PARENTING Program. For further insights into the process of Self-Parenting, read each book recommended in Chapter 12. But remember, the way you will be reading these books is based on your knowledge of Self-Parenting. The recommended books were written for a different purpose by their authors. You are reading them to apply the information contained in the books to your understanding of Self-Parenting. Once you understand the Self-Parenting concept, you can learn from many different sources.

For further sources of questions to ask during your sessions, you can order the beginning modules such as *Self-Esteem or Early Family and Childhood* from the SELF-PARENTING Program.

Follow Through

There are several different ways to follow through with a SELF-PARENTING Support Group.

1. You may continue to keep only the first meeting of each month open to newcomers and continue to follow the recommended format. A second group can be organized on another night for the advanced practitioners.
2. Your original group may choose to extend your meeting as a closed meeting for two (or more) months and use an introductory or advanced module for sharing as the basis of your meeting. (Each person must have his or her own module.)
3. This book has been designed as a study guideline to conduct advanced meetings. Simply read a chapter or section each week and discuss the principles in conjunction with your daily sessions.
4. You may also use a book, such as *Parent Effectiveness Training* by Thomas Gordon, and read one or more chapters a week and discuss the underlying application to Self-Parenting within the group. (This generally takes longer than a month.)

Once you begin the meetings and start sharing your experiences with other practitioners, you will discover many methods of gaining practical insights on the Self-Parenting process.

WORKING WITH A THERAPIST

Asking for help when you are confused or unsure is not a sign of weakness. It takes courage and strength to confront a fearful or doubtful situation by asking for guidance. Seeking help when you need it is a sign of positive Self-Parenting. Although this is the role of the Inner Parent, it is often the Inner Child who initiates the cry for help after being frustrated or thwarted for too long. If you have trouble with Self-Parenting on your own, you may benefit from working with a therapist.

When you are interviewing a potential therapist, ask, "Are you practicing daily half-hour sessions of Self-Parenting with your Inner Child?" If the answer is "No, but I understand Self-Parenting perfectly," this is not the optimum sign. The intellectual precepts of Self-Parenting are easy for a therapist to grasp. However, the therapists who wholeheartedly endorse Self-Parenting and even teach it to their clients but do not practice sessions cannot be as effective as those who do. How can you preach what you don't practice? The deeper understanding and experience of Self-Parenting can only be gained from practice.

We have had reports from many practitioners working with a therapists who didn't practice daily sessions. Most of them were already in therapy when they learned about Self-Parenting. Once they began sessions, they would tell their therapists about their sessions. Within three months of practice, their therapy time turned into just reading their Self-Parenting sessions to the therapists and having them say, "Great!" Practitioners felt that they had already transcended the therapists' ability to make meaningful contributions to their growth. This is especially interesting since some of these practitioners had been going to their therapists for several years. What had they been doing all that time?

The SELF-PARENTING Program maintains a list of support group contacts and therapists who work with practitioners. These therapists are professionals who have contacted us saying they follow and use the methods and techniques of the SELF-PARENTING Program. Contact the main office for a listing in your area. The address for the SELF-PARENTING Program is listed in the back of this book.

If there is no therapist listed in your area who is familiar with Self-Parenting, try giving your current therapist a copy of the book *SELF-PARENTING* and ask them if they would be willing to work with you. Although this is not the best solution, it may work out okay.

The main thing to remember is that it is up to *YOU* to practice daily half-hour sessions with your Inner Child. Without this, all the talking and counseling in the world won't make a lasting change in your Self-Parenting style.

THREE-MONTH ACHIEVEMENT

From the outside looking in, people have differing perceptions about Self-Parenting — what it is, what it does, what it is "just like." But for those on the inside looking out, there is a remarkably similar perspective. By practicing the SELF-PARENTING Program, you can experience something you have never experienced in any other way: the ongoing power and intimacy of a conscious, one-to-one relationship with your Inner Child.

People who don't practice half-hour sessions of Self-Parenting are not going to feel this power. They may imagine they are connected to their Inner Child. They might even assure you how much they are "in touch" with their Inner Child. But the proof is in the practice. As any practitioner will tell you, there is a big difference between practicing half-hour sessions and not practicing half-hour sessions.

Whether or not you engage in conscious half-hour sessions with your Inner Child, you are still Self-Parenting (unconsciously) inside your mind. Nothing changes in that regard. Although some people can be remarkably aware of their Inner Child, most individuals are Self-Parenting inside their Inner Conversations without any conscious awareness of this process.

One point is clear, however, no matter who you are or how advanced you have become in personal growth, after practicing conscious and directed half-hour sessions of positive Self-Parenting, you will become even more aware of this experience inside your mind.

Three Months

Three months is the approximate amount of time required before your Inner Child will experience the foundation of trust and security that comes from practicing daily half-hour sessions. Your first breakthrough is simply starting sessions. The next level occurs around three months, the next after one year. Each time frame brings significantly deeper levels of appreciation for your Self-Parenting process.

One principle to keep in mind during your first three months is that a beginning Self-Parenting student is a beginning Self-Parenting student. It is not possible to accomplish three months of practice in three weeks. It will take one full year of daily half-hour sessions to reach the one-year point. Your awareness and understanding as an Inner Parent will continue to improve three weeks, three months, three years from now. If you follow the proven guidelines, your pace is possible to predict and your progress is guaranteed.

Bonding With Your Inner Child

Many people who don't practice sessions believe that "getting in touch" with the Inner Child is the key issue in Self-Parenting. However, getting in touch with your Inner Child does not necessarily mean that healing follows automatically. In fact, for most people, getting in touch with their Inner Child will make them aware of neglect and abuse they have been trying to deny all their lives. Initial contact with your Inner Child is only the first step in a progressive process of changing the Inner Parent from a negative to a positive Self-Parenting style. One example of the role Self-Parenting can play for people in this regard is illustrated by the process biologists call bonding.

Baby mammals are biologically directed to stay close to their mothers. This is especially true when they are hungry, frightened or ill. This interaction is extremely physical and takes place through proximity, touching and physical play. Face-to-face interaction between human infants and their mothers serves to establish the foundation for the development of human interaction and communication skills.

Many men and women in modern society have never experienced this sense of bonding. Since they did not have an experience of emotional contact with their parents as children, they do not have this experience of contact between their Inner Parent and Inner Child. Since bonding is fundamental to the experience of positive Self-Parenting, lack of bonding is a serious problem.

A unique aspect of the SELF-PARENTING Program is that half-hour sessions initiate and establish a bonding process between the Inner Parent and Inner Child. Once people begin to experience this bonding process, they realize it has always been missing in their lives. When they discover the importance of this connection to their Inner Child, they gain a new appreciation for the practice of Self-Parenting. This is only one of the reasons that half-hour sessions are more valuable than speaking your Inner Conversations out loud to a therapist who is "guiding" you.

Half-hour sessions present a very effective tool for dealing with a lack-of-bonding problem. Daily sessions sustained over a period of several months will replace feelings of emptiness, which have been called the "hole in the soul." The accumulation of sessions over time will bring you a lasting sense of peace and fulfillment. Practicing half-hour sessions for three to six months will restore this sense of bonding with your Inner Child, as thousands of Self-Parenting practitioners can testify.

As an Inner Parent, you can make hundreds of mistakes a day. But there does come a point, usually after you have been doing half-hour sessions for about three months, when your Inner Child is won over. Because of the bonding that has taken place during your sessions, it becomes easier for the Inner Child to overlook and forgive the frequent mistakes you make as the Inner Parent. Daily half-hour sessions demonstrate in a real way that you care, that you are trying and that you are thinking about the needs of your Inner Child. When your Inner Child reaches this understanding, your Self-Parenting has reached a significant milestone.

4

RESOLVING YOUR INNER CONFLICTS

The Problem

Inner Conflicts are the least understood and most difficult problem area for the Self-Parenting practitioner. You can be stuck within an Inner Conflict for hours, days or weeks if you don't recognize that your Inner Child and Inner Parent are fighting.

The Solution

As the Inner Parent you must be ever vigilant for the signs and symptoms of an Inner Conflict. If you notice these signs, you can use the Eight Steps of Inner Conflict Resolution to successfully resolve the Inner Conflict with a Win/ Win solution.

INNER CONFLICT ISSUES

You have probably had the experience of wanting something with one part of your mind and wanting something else with the other part. In Self-Parenting, this is called an Inner Conflict. An Inner Conflict represents a power struggle between you and your Inner Child. The fewer Inner Conflicts you have the better, but it is impossible to avoid them altogether.

Everyone has Inner Conflicts; they are as much a part of everyday life as bad weather. So it is better to learn to anticipate and handle Inner Conflicts rather than ignore them or pretend they don't exist. What either self wants is usually a good idea for both selves in the long run. Therefore it is crucial to be well versed in problem-solving skills and to never accept anything less than a Win/Win resolution between the two Inner Selves.

Learning to recognize and resolve Inner Conflicts is one of the most important and valuable aspects of Self-Parenting. Inner Conflicts sound an alarm whenever your needs are not being met. Without a doubt, the successful handling of Inner Conflicts separates the novice from the serious Self-Parenting practitioner.

Part of the complexity of Inner Conflicts is that this is one area of Self-Parenting in which you can (and must) engage your Inner Child consciously outside your regular session. Even though dialogue with your Inner Child is not recommended outside your session during the first three months, Inner Conflicts create a true emergency situation, and emergencies must be handled immediately.

As mentioned earlier, dialogue with your Inner Child outside your sessions can get you into trouble. Even though you have good intentions as the Inner

Parent, you may take the new-found discovery of your Inner Child and unknowingly use your old, negative Self-Parenting style to dialogue with it. Your Inner Child naturally resists this intrusion, especially after experiencing the happiness and freedom that takes place during your sessions. Therefore, each attempt by the unskilled Inner Parent to engage in conscious dialogue outside the session can confuse your Inner Conversations even more.

The simplest way to avoid this problem is to practice resolving your Inner Conflicts on paper. The more you do this, the better your Inner Conflict resolution will become. The Inner Conflict procedures will protect your Inner Child by ensuring that you are a positive Inner Parent. Gradually, as you continue sessions and keep improving your Self-Parenting style, you will become much more aware of your Inner Child outside your sessions.

If you do experience an Inner Conflict outside your sessions (and you will), it will feel like a raging war with both sides suffering heavy casualties. In this situation, you will be armed with the Eight-Step procedure for resolving Inner Conflicts.

How to Tell When You Are Experiencing An Inner Conflict

Awareness of an Inner Conflict usually begins with physical or mental sensations that start affecting your body. Something is going wrong. You don't feel "normal." You will begin to notice a racing Inner Conversation circulating continuously inside your mind throughout all your activities. This Inner Conflict continues to increase in intensity until eventually you are immobilized due to the constant thinking and recurring body symptoms.

When this happens, you, as the Inner Parent, will have to do something to feel better. If you don't, the Inner Conflict could immobilize your mind and body for hours, days or weeks. Your Inner Child is unable to help because it doesn't know how. This would be like asking a child to handle a family emergency like a fire or a financial problem. People from the outside world can't help you because they can't hear your Inner Conversations. *Your Inner Parent must take charge to resolve an Inner Conflict.*

The key to resolving Inner Conflicts is to determine the needs of both Inner Selves and meet those needs with a Win/Win solution. You do this by following a procedure known as the Eight-Step Inner Conflict Resolution Process. These are the eight steps:

1. Your Inner Parent recognizes the physical signs of an Inner Conflict.
2. You write out your complete Inner Conversation, exactly as you hear it.
3. You fill out the Inner Conflict Master statement and list the specific needs of each Inner Self.
4. Both Inner Selves mutually agree to resolve this situation with a Win/Win solution.
5. Both Inner Selves brainstorm for potential solutions to the Inner Conflict.
6. Both Inner Selves decide upon a mutually acceptable solution or compromise that best meets the needs of both selves.
7. Your Inner Parent and Inner Child put the potential solution into action.
8. Both Inner Selves evaluate the solution for workability and satisfaction.

Unfortunately, in the typical Inner Conflict the unaware or untrained Inner Parent unknowingly uses the Win/Lose method to resolve conflicts. This solution usually satisfies the short-term needs of the Inner Parent, but leaves the Inner Child feeling unfulfilled.

Sometimes the rebellious or strong-willed Inner Child will create a Lose/Win situation which means that it will be happy to the detriment of the Inner Parent. Of course, the worst possibility is that both selves arrive at a Lose/Lose situation in which neither self is happy.

Any solution other than the Win/Win option is unsatisfactory for the optimal functioning of both selves. Either self getting its own way at the expense of the other self invites future problems. The best thing about a Win/Win solution to an Inner Conflict is that *both selves get their way!* This often seems impossible at first, but with practice you will be able to solve all of your Inner Conflicts this way. The self-confidence and self-mastery you gain by working toward Win/Win solutions with your Inner Child will make each Inner Conflict resolution progressively easier.

Any time you have a severe Inner Conflict you will need to take each step, in sequence, to establish and fulfill the needs of both Inner Selves. These procedures are the same problem-solving methods that psychologists and negotiators have been using for years to resolve the conflicts in outer relationships. These proven methods have simply been adapted for resolving Inner Conflicts within your Inner Conversations.

THE EIGHT STEPS TO INNER CONFLICT RESOLUTION

Step One: Your Inner Parent recognizes the physical signs of an Inner Conflict.

Inner Conflicts begin with physical, emotional and mental signals. Your Inner Parent will recognize that your body, emotions or thoughts are becoming immobilized by inactivity, indecision, or a constant, heated Inner Conversation that remains unresolved. Until your Inner Parent consciously recognizes this condition and takes steps to correct it, your Inner Parent and Inner Child could do battle for hours or days.

As an individual you will have your own unique symptoms of an Inner Conflict which you must learn to identify. Some typical examples are:
- Racing thoughts
- Thinking constantly about the same situation
- Inability to sleep
- Overeating
- Feeling overly tired
- Queasy stomach
- Sensation of fear or apprehension
- Pressure headaches
- Reluctance to do something you normally enjoy
- A sudden cold or unexpected illness
- Inability to make what seems like a simple decision

When you experience an Inner Conflict, you may have one or all of these signs or other physical symptoms that are specific to your own body. The important thing is to learn to quickly recognize the physical, emotional and mental sensations of your Inner Conflicts. The sooner you can recognize your personal signs of an Inner Conflict, the sooner you can begin the steps to resolve it.

Step Two: Write out your complete Inner Conflict exactly as you hear it.

After recognition, the next step is to *WRITE OUT YOUR INNER CONFLICT AS CLEARLY AND FULLY AS POSSIBLE.* The way you do this is to get several sheets of paper and start writing out *exactly* what you hear yourself saying inside your mind. This may seem difficult at first, but actually it is very easy. What you are saying inside your Inner Conversations is so strong, it will be easy to write it down *ONCE YOU BEGIN.*

Write out what you are thinking and feeling in the split-page format that you use during your sessions. Draw a line down the center of the sheet. Start writing what one voice is saying exactly the way you hear it inside your mind.

> *I don't want to go to grandmother's house. I don't care who will be there or why. The last time we went there . . . etc.*

Then, when that side is finished, there will be an opposing voice with its opinion. Skip down a line, switch sides of the paper, and start writing out the response.

I don't care what you say. We need to go because everyone is expecting us to be there. If we don't show up there will be hell to pay . . . etc.

Be sure to drop down a line each time you switch sides, and keep going until you have written down *everything* you are thinking and feeling about that subject. You must take the time during Step Two to write down your entire Inner Conversation carefully and completely. The more completely you can write down what you hear inside your mind using the split-page format, the sooner you will get it out of your mind and onto paper.

Don't be concerned if what you are writing sounds negative. If there are some swear words or insults involving friends or family members — so be it. You must record your Inner Conflict *exactly* as you hear it. Until someone invents a computer that can do this job, you will have to rely on your own listening and writing skills.

Also, you don't have to know in advance which voice is which before you begin. After you review what you have written, you will be able to separate easily the Inner Parent voice from the Inner Child.

A difficult Inner Conflict may take as long as 45 to 90 minutes to write out. If you think that is too long, think about how deeply this Inner Conflict must be affecting you if it takes that long to write down. For the most part, however, the intensity of a true Inner Conflict is so absorbing that writing it out seems to take only minutes, no matter how much clock time goes by.

Once you are all "written out," you will certainly feel a sense of relief. More importantly, you will find the Inner Conflict much easier to resolve for three reasons:

1. The inner turmoil lessens considerably once the Inner Conflict is written down because the conflict is out of your mind and onto the paper.
2. It will be much easier to determine which voice is which when you see the pattern of conversation coming from both sides of your mind. This often reveals the situation in an unusual way.
3. Sometimes the clarity you experience from writing down the Inner Conflict solves your problem on the spot.

If you have a deep-seated or long-standing issue, the same Inner Conflict may pop up in various forms over a period of days, weeks or months. In this case, you will be conducting many Inner Conflict sessions.

Step Three: Fill out the Master Statement and list the specific needs of each Inner Self.

Your Inner Conflict involves a conflict of needs between your two selves, but sometimes it is difficult to determine what those needs are unless the Inner Conversation is written out in an objective manner. Writing down your Inner Conflict on paper — in your own handwriting — separates and clarifies the demands of both selves. This process makes it easier for you to determine objectively what needs underlie the arguments of the two selves.

You will be much more aware of the many possible needs of the Inner Child after reading the section on *Needs* later in the book. In fact, you may want to refer to that section when working out a particularly difficult Inner Conflict. But in general, the primary needs of your Inner Child can be categorized as physical, emotional, mental or social. One or more of these basic needs will always underlie even the most outrageous demands or wants of your Inner Child.

Your next step is to complete the Master Statement of Inner Conflicts. Filling in the blanks to this statement will help you determine if you have a true conflict. This will be further explained in the following chapter. If you don't have a conflict within your Master Statement, you don't have an Inner Conflict. *WITHOUT A CONFLICT THE REST OF THE STEPS WON'T WORK.* Therefore, this step is vitally important.

To fill out the Master Statement, simply fill in the blanks.

My Inner Child wants to _____
and
My Inner Parent wants to _____ .

When completing the Master Statement, simply fill in the most obvious desire of each self. In the above example, it was:

My Inner Child wants to <u>not go to Grandmother's house</u>
and
My Inner Parent wants to <u>attend the family function.</u>

After you have filled out the Master Statement, you will have to make an evaluation to determine if your situation is a true Inner Conflict. *ONLY IF THE MASTER STATEMENT CONTAINS MUTUALLY OPPOSING OPTIONS DO YOU HAVE AN INNER CONFLICT.* For example:

My Inner Child wants to go shopping
and
My Inner Parent wants to stay home and catch up on reading.

My Inner Child wants to clean the car
and
My Inner Parent wants to go out and enjoy the weekend.

My Inner Parent wants to visit a friend in the hospital
and
My Inner Child wants to stay home and sleep.

My Inner Child wants to go to a picnic
and
My Inner Parent wants to stay home and watch sports.

My Inner Child wants to call an old boyfriend/girlfriend
and
My Inner Parent wants to remain out of contact.

My Inner Child wants to go shopping
and
My Inner Parent knows it has to go out and look for a job.

Each sentence in the above pairs of Master Statements is mutually exclusive. Both wants or desires cannot be met at the same time; they are mutually exclusive. This means you have a true Inner Conflict.

If you determine that you have an Inner Conflict, then follow the remaining steps to resolve it. If you can't find a specific and opposing conflict using the Master Statement, you have discovered one thing: you don't have a true Inner Conflict. The next chapter will discuss some situations in which the

Master Statement does not reveal a direct conflict. Assuming however that it does, the next part of Step Three will more closely determine the specific needs of each self.

The best way to completely list the needs of both Inner Selves is to start a new sheet of paper with a line down the middle. The left side will be for the needs of the Inner Parent, the right side for the needs of the Inner Child. The easiest way to determine the needs is to go back and read through what you have written and write down what each voice wants as you come to it.

As you read through what you have written it will be easy for you to tell what your Inner Parent wants and what your Inner Child wants. (If you still can't decide, show what you have written to a friend or support group member — they'll tell you which is which!) Write in what each self says it wants in the situation under the appropriate heading. For example:

My Inner Parent Wants to	**My Inner Child Wants to**
Go the family gathering	Stay Home
Bring a nice present for Lisa	Tell Joe where to go
Get there in time for the cake	Buy some new swim fins
Make a good impression	Watch a particular television show

By reading through your written sheets, you will be able to pick the specific desires that appear in your Inner Conflict. Write the specific demands of each self as they appear on the sheet onto your list. As both sides must have their needs met to resolve your Inner Conflict, Step Three begins the return of your Inner Conversations to their normal, happy and productive state.

Step Four: Both Inner Selves mutually agree to resolve this situation with a Win/Win solution.

Once the opposing needs of both sides are clear, the two selves must agree to support each other to help satisfy those needs. Sometimes this is the hardest step when it could be the easiest. The Inner Parent is often unwilling to give in to the demands of the Inner Child because they seem so outrageous. Neither self wants to give up its desire to win at any cost. What both selves have to realize is that *THEY ARE BOTH GOING TO WIN.*

Often both sides of the conflict believe it is impossible for their side to win without the other losing. Being stubborn this way is what keeps the conflict going. Until both Inner Selves can agree that there is at least a possibility that they both could win, you won't be able to continue with the next four steps. Sometimes only the Inner Parent can keep the faith and insist on this step as part of the resolution process.

Step Five: Both Inner Selves make a general search for potential solutions to the Inner Conflict.

This is the art of the deal. The way to proceed is to generate as many ideas as possible to accomplish and accommodate the needs of each Self during this step. Using the two-column sheet with the needs and desires of each self, list as many solutions as possible which will make either self happy. List any solution, even if it seems impractical or goes against the other self. For example:

Solutions For the Inner Parent	Solutions For Inner Child
Force the Inner Child to go using threats	Send Lisa's present UPS via next day air
Try to bribe the Inner Child using the swim fins	Fake getting sick
Have the family gathering at their house	Call the IRS on Joe
Hire a limousine for the drive	Buy a cake at the local bakery
	Call a friend to kidnap you on that day

The key to Step Five is creative brainstorming. During Step Five none of the solutions has to be decided on; they just need to be considered and written down. Each self can generate selfish solutions that will only help its side. Generating as many solutions as possible during this step stirs the creative juices of both selves. Even if the solutions are crazy or impractical, thinking this way will get the two selves working together.

This is another excellent point at which to show your needs list to a friend (or call a support group member) to see what suggestions he or she can come up with to meet the needs of the two Inner Selves.

Step Six: Choose a mutually acceptable solution or compromise that best meets the needs of both selves.

Through the ideas generated in Step Five, some solution or combination of ideas will emerge that both your Inner Parent and Inner Child can get excited about. This may be a true Win/Win solution or a choice that boils down to a difficult compromise for both sides. Nevertheless, if all angles and creative ideas have been explored, the solution or compromise will be mutually agreeable to both selves as the best possible solution at that time for that situation.

You may find during Step Five that all you need to solve your Inner Conflict is some information which you don't have at the time. If so, talk to your friends, go to the library or call your travel agent to see if the route can be changed. Be willing to do whatever it takes to find answers and potential solutions for the needs of both selves.

Step Seven: Your Inner Parent and Inner Child put the solution in motion.

This should be the easy part since both selves had a hand in evolving the solution and are optimistic about the outcome. However, you want to make sure that neither self lags if there are some specific tasks to be done that have been agreed upon. Many times the solution will require both selves to follow through on specific duties. Step Six represents a commitment to action that must be followed through in Step Seven.

Step Eight: Both selves evaluate the solution for workability and satisfaction.

Many times, your Inner Conflict will work itself out so quickly and easily that both selves will be amazed they were fighting in the first place! This is good news and congratulations are in order. In these circumstances the resolution is perfect and a problem that would have never gone away soon fades from memory. Once in a while, the solution doesn't work the way both selves hoped it would, or the outside circumstances change due to unforeseen influences or new information.

If this happens, all you have to do is repeat the Eight Steps and keep digging for that Win/Win solution. One Self-Parenting student (of six months) found herself in a major Inner Conflict. She spent a full day going through the Eight Steps and working out the perfect solution to her problem, or so she thought at the time. During her session two days later she realized her Inner Child must be having a problem. She had asked it 14 questions and received a one-word answer to each one!

On the 15th question, her Inner Child let her have it! The Inner Conflict resolution from two days before had been completely one-sided, according to her Inner Child. It complained for several pages that the Inner Parent had completely disregarded her needs. (Meanwhile, she was writing everything down and saying "Thank you, Inner Child, for telling me that!") Upon evaluation, the practitioner realized that indeed, as an Inner Parent, she had completely worked through the Eight-Step process without truly meeting her Inner Child's needs.

She went through the Eight Steps again. This time she was much more conscious of her Inner Child's side of the process. The moral of this story is that even experienced practitioners can make genuine mistakes. This problem was very deep. The fact that she eventually did resolve the situation satisfactorily was a tribute to her Inner Parent's willingness to seek the Win/Win solution *AND* to the process of Self-Parenting itself.

The good news is that each experience of resolving Inner Conflicts will smooth out and make future problem-solving much easier. With practice you will learn to head off Inner Conflicts before they arise. As you learn to cooperate with your Inner Child to resolve Inner Conflicts, a new confidence and trust will develop within your relationship. Both Inner Selves will learn to be more open and aware of each other's needs. As in every successful relationship, your Inner Parent and Inner Child will grow in understanding and commitment as they begin to communicate with each other more intimately.

FURTHER STRATEGIES FOR RESOLVING INNER CONFLICTS

As you practice the Eight Steps of Inner Conflict Resolution, you will find that each resolution of an Inner Conflict will give you experience and confidence. Eventually you will have a reduction in the frequency of your Inner Conflicts. You will also develop, through practical experience, some Self-Parenting strategies that will make your life easier living in the "real world."

For example, with some Inner Conflicts, you can simply give in to your Inner Child right away. What you, as the Inner Parent, are trying to prevent may not be that bad and you can let the Inner Child have what it wants without suffering. The peace of mind from giving up the hassle is worth it alone.

One good way to decide if you should just give in during an Inner Conflict is to ask yourself, "If a close friend wanted to do what my Inner Child wants to do, would I encourage and support them?" If the obvious answer is *YES,* then why are you, the Inner Parent, preventing your Inner Child from having the same experience? If your Inner Child is your best friend, why not give it what you would willingly allow your outer friends? Examples of this might be a trip to Hawaii, some special clothes or an offbeat vacation.

If you wouldn't encourage a friend to take this particular path because you consider it dangerous, foolhardy or a step backwards, then you must take the more difficult step of explaining the reasons to your Inner Child and attempting to fulfill its needs in a more acceptable way. (It works the same way for your friends, as well.) In this situation you would go through the eight-step procedure as usual.

When you are writing out your Inner Conflict, you will learn to recognize when the conflict will not cause the Inner Parent to feel that it loses if it doesn't get its way. In these circumstances, giving in early will save both selves much grief and hassle.

Sharing Your Inner Conflict

Many times you are so wrapped up with an Inner Conflict you can't see the forest for the trees. After you have written out your Inner Conflict completely, you might find it beneficial to show it to some friends who understand Self-Parenting. From their unbiased perspective, they will be able to quickly point you toward a solution that is a Win/Win resolution. This is also an excellent time for sharing in your support group or showing your therapist what you have written.

If your Inner Conflict involves a particular person, you might want to show the other person what you have written. Depending on the circumstances, you might want to ask your Inner Child if this would be okay. You must make sure that you protect your Inner Child from more hurt. If you think this person might use this information against you, letting them read your intimate thoughts and feelings is a bad idea.

If the other person indicates they would like to understand you better, let them read what you have written. Having someone read your deepest thoughts and feelings is an excellent way for you to share and communicate without the pressure of a face-to-face confrontation. This also gives you a starting point for resolving the issue. If the person is not interested in reading your Inner Conflict about your relationship, your relationship is in trouble.

Quick Decision-Making for Minor Inner Conflicts

Here is a method to make a quick choice in a situation that demands a quick response. This is practical when the issue is a minor Inner Conflict, but you are still unsure about what to do. You know you have an Inner Conflict, but it's too minor for the full eight-step procedure.

For example, suppose a friend calls and asks you to go to a movie. You thought you might want to see this movie, but he has asked you on late notice and you are not sure what to do. You kind of want to go and you kind of want to stay home and simply watch television.

A good way to make a quick decision is to ask your Inner Child the following:

"Inner Child, on a scale of one to ten how much do you want to _____ ?"

This gives you a number between one and ten. If the number is five or below, don't do what you were planning. If the number is six or above, do it.

In this example you would tell your friend to hang on for a second. Then you ask your Inner Child inside your mind,

"Inner Child, on a scale of one to ten how much do you want to go to this movie tonight?"

If the answer is five or less, then you know your Inner Child does not want to give you the energy for that choice. Even if you force your Inner Child to comply, you will not enjoy yourself or you will feel worse for going when you get home. If you are still unsure, you could ask another question based on your second option:

"Inner Child, on a scale of one to ten how much do you want to stay home and watch (the television show) tonight?"

Usually this will yield an even higher or lower answer that helps you to decide immediately. To use this technique most effectively, just ask your Inner Child the "scale of one to ten" question using both choices.

Personal Crises

Other problems can give your Inner Conversations the stress and strain signals of an Inner Conflict. Another situation that creates immediate racing

Inner Conversations and thus seems like an Inner Conflict is a personal crisis. This is a traumatic event that rudely thrusts itself into your life, such as an earthquake or the sudden death or suicide of a family member.

Personal crises come from outside; they are external circumstances. They are not self-inflicted problems such as making a bad decision or forgetting to pay your car insurance. They are unexpected circumstances that disrupt your smooth plans, or they may be accidental situations that happen to others which negatively affect your life.

Times of personal crisis call for a boost in positive Self-Parenting. If the crisis is very serious, your best bet may be to put yourself into the hands of someone capable and go completely into your Inner Child to grieve. Let a trusted friend or therapist be your surrogate parent. Let their job be to love, support and nurture you unconditionally; let your job be to express and release your emotions. If you do experience a personal crisis, you can still use Self-Parenting techniques to parent yourself positively.

Write out your Inner Conversations about the crisis — get them out of your mind by releasing them onto a piece of paper. Don't worry about which voice is which, just write down everything you hear inside your mind as quickly and completely as you can. Always keep this principle in mind — externalizing your inner turmoil onto paper causes it to weaken or be re- solved. During a time of personal crisis you can write at any time outside your session.

After your Inner Conversations are out of your mind and onto the paper, you will feel better for venting and releasing. If you are drained, take a break and relax. If this is a serious crisis, more feelings and emotions will surface in time. Just keep repeating the process of writing out your Inner Conversations several times in the next few hours or days. When you feel sick and tired of hurting so much, you will have reached the turning point.

Even as you begin to feel better, you may realize that you are developing another racing Inner Conversation. This one may be yet another feeling or perspective about the same crisis or a related issue. Perhaps it reminds you of an earlier situation when you had the same feelings. Be sure to write this down as well. Even though you have written out 7 to 20 Inner Conversations and you feel much better, don't let one negative feeling linger or you may remain only "slightly depressed" for days.

You may also realize during the course of writing about a personal crisis that you actually do have an Inner Conflict. In this case follow the Eight Steps of Inner Conflict Resolution.

Breaking Bad Habits

Attempting to break a long-term habit can be tricky, even with Self-Parenting. There is no single rule for changing old patterns. Sometimes a gradual change in routine is better for the Inner Child, and sometimes the "cold turkey" approach is more effective. Correcting bad habits is a profound area of Self-Parenting awareness in which you are often on your own. You can ask the experts for advice, read all the books and still you and your Inner Child must go through the process together to reach your own Win/Win solution.

Here is one hint: your Inner Child will learn new rules, but only if you enforce them. When both you and your Inner Child accept, know and follow the rules, arguments and tension will be reduced. After all, you, as the Inner Parent, do not want to devote most of your energy to rigid self-control.

A delicate balance exists between the Inner Parent and Inner Child when creating change. It is best to proceed cautiously when trying to establish new routines in your life. Trying to change all your bad habits after one week of Self-Parenting can backfire. Overeating, smoking, coffee drinking and other questionable practices can be complicated Self-Parenting issues.

During your early months of Self-Parenting, you are better off simply enjoying the interaction between you and your Inner Child rather than trying to change long-term habits that you might not yet understand in terms of their Self-Parenting dynamics. Often bad habits that you have been trying to get rid of for years will simply drop away after a few months of regular sessions with your Inner Child. Many Self-Parenting practitioners have testified to this.

"INNER BASHINGS"

During the early stages of improving your Self-Parenting style, you may try to resolve what you think is an Inner Conflict but it doesn't seem to work. You are certain you have an Inner Conflict because you are experiencing mental anguish, body symptoms and a nonstop Inner Conversation. Because of this, you begin the process of following the Eight Steps of Inner Conflict Resolution. Yet when you reach Step Three and try to fill out the Master Statement, you do not find a direct conflict of needs. When this happens, you are most likely experiencing a category of Self-Parenting interaction we call an "Inner Bashing."

Inner Bashings seem to be more of a blaming or a name-calling contest between the two Inner Selves, rather than a true attempt by either self to resolve a conflict. You are experiencing an ongoing, negative Inner Conversation that is not about a specific subject but is simply a vague, recurring series of complaints. If writing out your Inner Conflict has shown that there is no direct conflict of needs, this means you have some more detective work to perform as the Inner Parent.

We have encountered many instances of Inner Bashings in our support groups. Here is a typical one:

TYPICAL INNER BASHING AT A SUPPORT GROUP MEETING

Inner Parent	Inner Child
We need to go to work to make money.	
	I don't want to go to work, I hate my job.

You are lazy and stupid. If you would work harder we could get more done. Then we could get out of this job.

It's not my fault. If you would do what I said six months ago we would be working over at _____ already. You're the one who is lazy and stupid.

We can't quit here because we will need first and last months' rent at the new place, and we can't do that because you won't get your butt in gear. You are holding back energy.

Yeah? Well, you forgot to (blah, blah, blah). You are an idiot.

That wasn't my fault. You should have reminded me. That was a dumb idea anyway.

Various name-calling, expletives, etc.

Various name-calling, expletives, etc.

Another version of an "Inner Bashing" occurs when the Inner Child seems to complain endlessly during sessions about the Inner Parent. This situation is very difficult for the Inner Parent to deal with when the Inner Child continually makes comments such as:

You are lazy.
Get it together.
When are you going to love me?
I don't believe you.
That's what you promised last time.
Don't give me that _____ again.
That's your job.
I can't stand this pressure any more.
You're a bad Inner Parent.

These never-ending negative complaints are confusing because you feel intense emotions coming from your Inner Child, yet you are trying your best to love, support and nurture it. This negative attitude from the Inner Child is immobilizing in itself. This is why "Inner Bashings" are often mistaken for Inner Conflicts by new practitioners.

This situation seems to occur frequently among practitioners who have a weak Inner Parent. If you are experiencing this situation in your half-hour sessions, your sessions can be boring or difficult. It may be a hardship to sit down for your daily session rather than a pleasure. The following real-life examples can give you some guidelines for evaluating your sessions to determine if you are suffering from an Inner Bashing.

INNER BASHINGS ARE DIAGNOSED ON THE BASIS OF THE MASTER STATEMENTS YOU FILL OUT IN STEP THREE OF THE INNER CONFLICT RESOLUTION. A true Inner Conflict must be a disagreement between the two Inner Selves on the same subject that seems irreconcilable on the surface. If your statements are not disagreements on the same subject or are not mutually exclusive, you do not have a direct conflict. The following situations are more likely to be "Inner Bashings" because the Master Statement indicates no true conflict of needs.

My Inner Child is complaining about life in general
and
My Inner Parent is frustrated and doesn't know what to do about it.

My Inner Child hates me as an Inner Parent
and
My Inner Parent is trying but seems to make matters worse.

My Inner Parent wants to go to Santa Barbara
and
My Inner Child wants to complain about the Inner Parent.

My Inner Child wants to open up a new business
and
My Inner Parent wants to talk about taking a trip to Boston.

My Inner Child hates going to work
and
My Inner Parent needs money for expenses.

Even the last example (a particularly common one) doesn't quite get down to the conflict level. Sure, the Inner Child doesn't want to go to work, and the Inner Parent needs money. That *sounds* like a conflict. But the trouble with this "conflict" is that the conversation is not specific enough. The Inner Child may not want to go to work, but what does it want to do instead?

Another clue: what exactly is it that the Inner Child hates about going to work? How does the Inner Parent going to work frustrate the needs of the Inner Child, whatever those are? Does the Inner Child have a need for sleep because it has been working 18 hour days for six straight weeks? Or does it have a need to visit a new girlfriend? Vague statements like the last example might not be about work at all, but about some long-standing problem in the person's Self-Parenting style which has not been uncovered.

An "Inner Bashing" is also easy to determine by reading it in front of your support group. No one in your group will be able to tell what either self wants, and they will be as confused as you are. This means that what both selves are saying doesn't really make sense as a conflict, and therefore you are bashing yourself inside your mind.

The best solution for resolving an "Inner Bashing" is for you to stop what you are saying as the Inner Parent and simply listen and accept what the Inner Child says without judgment. If your Inner Child is calling you names, simply respond, "Thank you, Inner Child, for telling me that." By listening in this way you will stop the endless loop of negativity.

If your Inner Child continues to complain, you may want to ask further questions during your half-hour sessions. Each day of sessions will continue to improve your relationship and the problem will eventually disappear. These situations are usually similar to the nagging mother who is continually commenting about the child's actions. Only when she shuts up will the child be allowed to live in peace.

PROBLEM SESSIONS

Some practitioners experience what could be called "problem sessions." These are stagnant sessions that don't seem to go anywhere. This section will give you some guidelines to help you determine what might be causing this situation. Your half-hour sessions should be a pleasant and positive experience most of the time. If they are not, the Inner Parent needs to investigate what it is doing incorrectly.

Many times the quality of your session is affected because the Inner Parent is asking "pre-loaded" questions. In other words, the Inner Parent begins the question by assuming that it knows what the Inner Child feels. The only problem is that the Inner Child might not feel that way at all!

For example, one practitioner's Inner Parent was "in love" with a man we'll call Bill. She automatically ascribed feelings of "love" and "attraction" to her Inner Child for him, when in reality her Inner Child didn't care about him at all. Yet, because she was a dominant Inner Parent, she would base an entire session on "her feelings" about Bill.

If she had only asked her Inner Child, "How do you feel about Bill?" she would have received an honest answer. But instead she asked, "Inner Child, what is it about Bill you miss the most?" or "Inner Child, what does Bill give you that other boyfriends don't?" In order to please and placate her Inner Parent, the Inner Child answered the question by making up feelings.

Another practitioner asked her Inner Child, "Why are you afraid of quitting work?" In fact, the Inner Child wasn't afraid of quitting work, it was the Inner Parent who was afraid of quitting work. Based on the way she asked her question, she was unconsciously assuming that the Inner Child shared this emotion.

Asking pre-loaded questions confuses the Inner Child by assuming in advance what it is feeling, thus complicating your sessions. When your Inner Child is told what to feel, it will often try to cooperate with you by feeling that way.

To avoid this, both new and advanced practitioners can use a very simple series of three questions. Using this three-question process as a departure point for daily sessions is a very effective method for bringing up a subject to discuss in a way that the Inner Child accepts. Your sessions won't get boring, and they will be more effective from the Inner Parent's perspective as well.

The three questions are:

1. *Inner Child, what would you like to talk about today?*

   Response of the Inner Child.

2. *TY — Inner Child, what about (the situation)?*

   Response of the Inner Child.

3. *TY — Inner Child, what is your need?*

   Response of the Inner Child.

The first question invites the Inner Child to talk about any subject it chooses. If it is Bill, so be it. Whether it's laundry, cleaning the house or moving to Hawaii, it doesn't really matter.

The second question draws out the particular aspect of this subject that the Inner Child would like to discuss. It may become a slightly different line of discussion that leads to an entirely different subject area, or it may be exactly what the Inner Parent thought it was. Either way, you are approaching the subject from the Inner Child's perspective, not the Inner Parent's. This is a very positive act for the Inner Parent because it supports the Inner Child's choice for a communication subject.

The third question allows the Inner Child to tell you what its needs are concerning the topic under discussion. For example, you are talking about an upcoming vacation with your Inner Child and the response to question three is:

> *I want to rent a motor scooter and take a ride in the country.*

Then you know the Inner Child has told you its need concerning this situation. This method is very effective for finding out what your Inner Child wants to say concerning the multitude of topics you might discuss during your sessions. Begin your daily sessions this way instead of pre-loading your questions about "Bill" or "quitting work." It will also prevent your sessions from becoming boring or stagnant.

Another hint — don't open your session by asking, "Inner Child, how are you *FEELING* today?" Many Inner Parents use this approach, but this question with its emphasis on *FEELINGS* sets up an expectation for your Inner Child to produce some *FEELINGS* to make the Inner Parent happy. Again, this is a form of pre-loading your questions.

You will do much better to simply ask your Inner Child more open-ended questions such as:

"Inner Child, how are you today?"
"Inner Child, how are you doing right now?"
"Inner Child, how's it going?"
"Inner Child, is there anything you want to tell me before we begin this session?"
"Inner Child, did you enjoy _____ last night?"

Asking open-ended questions in this way will allow your Inner Child more freedom to respond. Your Inner Child can often surprise you with feelings or insights that you had no idea it had.

Boring Sessions

At various times, your sessions may become boring for both Inner Selves. No one wants boring sessions. If this is happening to you, it is a sign that your Inner Parent is stagnating. The positive Inner Parent will need to maintain an active interest in keeping the energy moving during sessions.

This is similar to the way a teacher must keep an active and interesting curriculum for his or her students. If not, the students will become bored and turned off to the class and the teacher.

If you find that your sessions become boring, you must do something as an Inner Parent to get out of your rut. The occasional boring session is okay. But if this becomes a pattern, you must take action as an Inner Parent to change the situation. One good policy, as discussed earlier, is to lead your sessions with the energy created by the current issues in your life. After reading The Opening, you can begin your session with the always popular, "Inner Child, how are you today?" If your Inner Child has nothing major to discuss, this might be a good opportunity to use one of the modules to explore some deeper issues.

Another way to break out of boring sessions is to ask a member of your support group (or your therapist) to read your sessions and give you feedback. Another important key can be to read recommended books on outer parenting for ideas to stimulate and educate your Inner Parent. Often you will need some outside help to get your sessions moving again. If you let boring sessions continue for too long, your Inner Child will eventually rebel and make your sessions difficult rather than pleasurable.

My Inner Child Won't Answer My Questions

New practitioners get confused by the ease of the SELF-PARENTING Program. More accurately, their Inner Parent underestimates the simplicity of Self-Parenting, thus adding unnecessary complications.

It seems so simple. Ask your Inner Child a question, write down its answer completely and then say, "Thank you, Inner Child, for telling me that." Yet people often complain that their Inner Child is not answering their question. When asked to read their session, it sounds something like this:

*"Inner Child, how did you feel
about the abuse you took as a child
in school?"*

The Inner Child replies . . .

"I don't want to answer that question."

Now remember, the practitioner's big complaint is that her Inner Child was not answering her question. She was very upset because her "sessions were not working." What she didn't seem to realize was that *her Inner Child was answering the question.* It was answering by saying that it didn't want to answer.

Before the deeper levels of trust can be established (such as by practicing ongoing Self-Parenting sessions for two years or more), you will often ask your Inner Child a question that it is just not willing to answer, not for you, not for anyone. If it responds to your question by stating that it doesn't want to answer your question, then *THIS IS ITS ANSWER!* It just may not be the answer that you, as the Inner Parent, are looking for. It would be wonderful to always get the exact answer that you want from your Inner Child, but this is not always possible.

Outer parents would love to get the exact answers they want from their outer children. Every husband and wife wants to receive the exact answer they are looking for from their spouse. Unfortunately, relationships don't work that way in the "real world." Your Inner Parent and Inner Child relationship is exactly that — a relationship between two different selves who often have difficulty communicating with each other.

Thank goodness we don't teach you to start off your sessions by saying:

*"Inner Child, I am going to ask you
some questions. I already know the
answers, but I just want to hear
them from you. So tell me the
answers you think I want to hear."*

Most of us don't want phony answers from our Inner Child. We get enough of that from other people. We want the deepest and truest answer from our Inner Child, to the best of its ability. But this is not always easy for the Inner Child. Your Inner Child may have been neglected or abused in very powerful ways. It may not be that anxious to open up its intimate feelings all of a sudden. It may require large doses of attention and acceptance for an extended period before it begins to trust you as the Inner Parent.

Here is another example that came from our workshops. Suppose you ask your Inner Child:

*"Inner Child what would you like
for lunch today?"*

And it says . . .

> *"I'm bored, I'm tired and I'm sick of
> this."*

You are getting an answer, but not a direct answer to your question. Since it does qualify as an answer we say, as always, "Thank you, Inner Child, for telling me that."

But you may have some room to move here. What would you do if you asked a co-worker what she wanted for lunch and she said, "I'm bored, I'm tired and I'm sick of this." You might wonder to yourself, "What?" but most likely you would accept her statement and ask the question again.

So, too, you can ask your Inner Child a question and if the answer seems a bit roundabout, just thank your Inner Child and repeat the question. *Don't be afraid to ask questions more than once.* As long as you are asking questions, you are still being a positive Inner Parent.

Here is the tricky part: don't get pushy. Your Inner Child may not want to answer a deeply personal question or it may not even know the answer! A vague, spurious or even completely wrong response is still your Inner Child's answer.

One new Self-Parenting practitioner (less than three months) told the following story. She was asking her Inner Child some very tough questions because she felt it "had an issue" and she wanted to get to the bottom of it. She pressed and pressured her Inner Child for an answer which did not come. Because it wouldn't answer her, she decided (as an Inner Parent) that she would go to a hypnotist to "get to the bottom" of the Inner Child's issue. Surprisingly, this also did not work.

Eventually her Inner Parent gave up and "decided" that it was okay for her Inner Child to have a secret issue and that she wouldn't pursue it any more. A few days later her Inner Child casually mentioned to her during a session,

> *"You didn't think, just because you've done a few Self-Parenting sessions with me, that I was going to trust you completely yet, did you?"*

Self-Parenting is not about playing games with your Inner Child. Your Inner Child is taking this work very seriously and is much more aware of what is actually going on with your sessions than you, the Inner Parent. If it doesn't want to answer your question the way you want it to, it probably has a good reason.

Always keep this fundamental teaching of the SELF-PARENTING Program in mind. Your Inner Child's answer is its answer. By saying, "Thank you, Inner Child, for telling me that," you grant dignity to your Inner Child's answer because you are listening to and accepting what your Inner Child tells you.

How Self-Parenting Works With Buried Or Repressed Issues

Some people ask the question, "How does Self-Parenting deal with unconscious or buried issues?" The answer is, "Very appropriately!" Here is a typical example.

A fairly new Self-Parenting practitioner was doing a session when his Inner Child mentioned that it wanted to listen to some Elvis Presley music. His Inner Parent thought that was a bit strange since they hadn't listened to Elvis for a long time, but he told his Inner Child, "Okay, no problem."

Later during the day, as the Elvis record was playing, his memory (the Inner Child) suddenly traveled back over 20 years to a romance he had when he was 17. His consciousness was flooded with the emotional feelings and memories of a certain girl. After thinking about her intensely and realizing that his feelings for her had never been resolved, he sat down and wrote her a ten-page letter. He apologized for his part in the relationship, thus clearing both Inner Selves of the guilt and sadness his Inner Child had been carrying (in a repressed form) ever since that time.

On the surface, his Inner Child had only made a tiny request to listen to some Elvis. Because the Inner Parent was paying attention, he granted the request, thinking only that it was rather odd. As a result of the openness and trust established through practicing half-hour sessions, the Inner Child's repressed emotions were allowed to surface and release. Also, because of the format of the Self-Parenting sessions, the practitioner's Inner Parent was receptive rather than suppressive or fearful of a major release of repressed emotions. Thus, the experience was allowed to take place, not rejected or denied as so often happens.

Imagine what would happen if you as the Inner Parent, after hearing about this case, began to play Elvis music during your sessions in order to stir up old memories and insisted that your Inner Child work on "issues with old girlfriends." It is doubtful that much emotional growth and release would be accomplished. Yet this is not unlike the process used by many therapists and psychological seminars.

Confrontational tactics and seminars are not necessarily bad. It's just that your Inner Child will respond more positively to a gentle, nurturing approach for excavating buried emotions. When the Inner Child is ready to release and the Inner Parent is able to pay attention and respond appropriately, a much more natural and gentle release can be achieved. This is preferable to the Inner Parent interrogating the Inner Child about "issues" which the Inner Child has neither the interest nor the willingness to examine.

Half-hour sessions provide many opportunities for your Inner Child to tell you about memories and feelings that have lain dormant for years. One module, *Early Family and Childhood,* is designed specifically for this purpose. The safe and supportive atmosphere of your half-hour session can be the ideal environment for exploring older issues. But a key concept of Self-Parenting is important to keep in mind: if you can love, support and nurture your Inner Child today concerning the current issues in your life, you will experience more happiness and peace of mind tomorrow than by trying to dredge up buried memories.

If you practice your sessions, and your Inner Child doesn't bring up any deeply buried emotions, fantastic! Just let it be and enjoy sharing this special interaction with your Inner Child. The Inner Parent who tries to pull information out of the Inner Child before it is ready is an Inner Parent with a negative Self-Parenting style. When your Inner Child wants to let go of a buried issue, it will do so in its own time, at its own pace. The best part is that you will be there waiting patiently as the Inner Parent, ready to say, "Thank you, Inner Child, for telling me that."

5

INTERMEDIATE PRACTITIONER GUIDELINES

The Problem

Sustaining the energy for ongoing sessions after six months can be difficult for some. The weak Inner Parent is usually the problem. If the Inner Parent is weak, it won't follow through on its recurring role to love, support and nurture the Inner Child.

The Solution

Intermediate practitioners must continue to educate and train the Inner Parent. Strengthening your Inner Parent outside your sessions is an important part of learning and honing your Self-Parenting skills. This chapter explores the process of Self-Parenting from many different perspectives based on the experiences of practitioners at the intermediate level.

INTERMEDIATE GUIDELINES

Changing your Self-Parenting style from negative to positive is a complex undertaking. You will experience many stages along the way. Based on feedback from thousands of practitioners, we can predict several stages as you make this transition. The guidelines in this chapter will be most applicable when you have been practicing half-hour sessions for at least six months. Depending on where you are with your half-hour sessions, the advice in these chapters can be a lifesaver.

During this intermediate stage the first process of change is awareness; then you realize you must make changes. As a result, you may experience periods of frustration as you come to realize how much you have neglected or abused your Inner Child in the past. The frustration comes as your awareness and responsibility as the Inner Parent increase.

Just after the new awareness begins and before the changes you have initiated can become permanent, there is a tendency for the Inner Parent to feel depressed. You know what you are doing wrong, but you can't seem to stop. You may feel pressure or self-doubt as an Inner Parent because you are not moving "fast enough." Even though you have been doing sessions for over six months, you feel that your life is just as bad as it was before sessions, maybe even worse. If this happens, rest assured that your life is not worse; you are simply becoming more aware.

The good news after practicing Self-Parenting for several months is that your Inner Child will become much more cooperative and loving. As the Inner Parent becomes more aware, the Inner Child can finally relax because it knows that the end of neglect and abuse is near. The Inner Child has a happy habit of forgiving the Inner Parent when it knows the Inner Parent is making a sincere effort to convert from negative to positive parenting. If your Inner Child knows you are depressed, it may even try to cheer you up!

Now that you have practiced sessions for a while, this is the time to think back to your life before you began half-hour sessions. Did you really know what Self-Parenting was? Even though you may have heard about the Inner Child and had been told to "pay attention to" or "learn to love" your Inner Child, did you really know what that meant? What changes occurred in your understanding of Self-Parenting after just three days of sessions? What types of transformative and exciting changes have come into your life as a result of continuing half-hour sessions? How many of these changes would have occurred from just reading books about your Inner Child?

Self-Parenting is a skill, like playing the piano. First you must learn the fundamentals of the piano and practice for many hours to develop familiarity with the keyboard. Once you have learned the basics, you can explore many styles or varieties of music.

Because conscious Self-Parenting is a skill-based activity, some people will find it easier than others. However, comparisons between one person and another have no meaning. What matters is the level of ability each person develops within his or her Self-Parenting style. With consistent practice, any person can improve their personal Self-Parenting skills if they have the desire.

Learning to improve your Self-Parenting skills is very much like learning any new skill; you have to practice. Fortunately, there is a fun and easy way to practice your Self-Parenting skills. Each day practitioners of the SELF-PARENT-ING Program practice communicating and interacting with their Inner Child for 30 minutes. These sessions give you many opportunities to improve and extend your Self-Parenting abilities. If you feel frustration as the Inner Parent, just think back to your life before Self-Parenting. That will cheer you up!

Little Things Count

When you first start Self-Parenting, the Inner Parent is often worried about the "big issues" such as where to work, whom to date or "why my parents treated me the way they did." It may take several months of half-hour sessions before you learn how much the power of the SELF-PARENTING Program applies to the little things. This represents an important guidepost to your progress.

You are making substantial gains in your Self-Parenting style when you begin to notice that your Inner Child wants to wear the red shoes instead of the black ones. Even though neither choice really matters as far as your career is concerned, the fact that you have heard your Inner Child express its choice is a major achievement. Or perhaps you notice after only three internal messages that you need to go to the bathroom. This may not seem very significant until you correlate this example to the outer parent who repeatedly ignores his or her child's requests to go to the bathroom.

The Quantum Level of Self-Parenting

Why do people have some of their happiest experiences and deepest levels of appreciation of Self-Parenting when they find out that they want one sugar in their coffee, not two? What is the reason, after a person hears the Inner Child suggest driving to work a different way, that he or she experiences a week of positive energy? These simple insights seem too trivial to produce such overwhelming effects. Here is the explanation, with a little help from modern physics.

Normal energy, the type you get from burning wood or paper, is called *molecular energy.* It heats up, it's hot, it's over. On the *molecular* level, different types of materials produce different rates of energy release. For example, you can burn wood but not sand.

However, on the deeper *quantum* level of energy, one pound of anything (sand, wood, Ping-Pong balls) will produce 11,400 million kilowatt-hours of energy. A pound of wood or a gallon of oil will provide a certain amount of energy on the *molecular* level. The same material on the *quantum* level gives you many thousands times that.

In a very similar way, this is what happens to practitioners of the Self-Parenting Program. Most people experience their lives on the outer level. They practice a procedure, take a seminar or learn a new skill. Someone outside themselves helps them or tells them what to do. Depending on the value of what they learn or are told, they benefit from the information.

The SELF-PARENTING Program takes you to a much deeper level of emotional and mental interaction. By dealing intimately with your own Inner Conversations you become aware at a much deeper and more powerful *quantum* level. When you perceive a subtle distinction at this level over a mundane subject such as which shoes to wear to work, you are releasing energies and power you never knew existed. This is why the daily practitioner gains so much energy and insight from Self-Parenting.

The key to the *quantum* level of Self-Parenting is that if you discover something for yourself, it is much more powerful and important than if someone else tells you. For example, there are many questions or issues in your life for which outsiders could give you the perfect solution. But if you receive this answer from within your own Inner Conversations, you will be much more motivated to follow through with the information.

Here is another example from the "real world." This book contains over 20 years of accumulated knowledge on the Self-Parenting process. If you read it ten times and had it memorized, you would still know less about Self-Parenting on a *quantum* level than a person who had practiced six week's worth of sessions.

The "To Do" List

Part of learning to be a positive Inner Parent at the intermediate level is learning to integrate what you discover from your sessions into your daily life. Once you have acquired some basic knowledge and experience, you can introduce advanced procedures into your daily practice. These tips represent an advanced application of the SELF-PARENTING Program. Let's start with an important one.

Often during your session your Inner Child will give you a great idea or offer a suggestion that is very appropriate to your life. You will, of course, write it down as part of your session, but you may forget this information as soon as the session is over, especially if the idea has nothing to do with the current session. If you don't review your session carefully, you may forget this great idea. As a result you will lose this valuable suggestion and your Inner Child will be upset (unconsciously) because it knows it told you but you, as the Inner Parent, didn't do anything about it.

This is why, at the intermediate user stage, it is appropriate to keep a separate "To Do" list at your side during your sessions. When your Inner Child gives you a suggestion or makes a request, write it down in the normal manner as part of your Self-Parenting role. Then, jot down the same sentence on a separate "To Do" list. Don't spend too much time elaborating on the idea; that is best done after the session. After your session, be sure to incorporate your notes into your daily "To Do" list. If you don't have a daily "To Do" list, now is the time to start!

Sometimes what your Inner Child says may or may not sound that important to you as the Inner Parent. Typical suggestions might be: "Let's go to a pet store," or "Don't forget to buy Lisa a birthday card," or "I want to have a seafood salad at lunch today." Yet you should definitely follow up on your Inner Child's suggestions just as if they were errands for family, social or work relationships. They are errands, but they are for your Inner Child.

The importance of these suggestions may not become apparent until you follow through on them and see how good you feel as a result. One practitioner was being nagged by her Inner Child to go to a pet store. This had been going on for a least a week or two. Because the Inner Parent was a busy executive and because she couldn't see any reason to go to a pet store, she did not make it a priority. One day during her session, she finally decided her Inner Child was important enough that she ought to create the time to visit the pet store. When she did, her Inner Child was overwhelmingly pleased in a way that she, as the Inner Parent, had not expected at all. She felt a deepening and more intimate relationship with her Inner Child as a result. Another *quantum* experience had occurred.

Review Your Sessions

It can be beneficial, especially after doing your sessions for six to eight weeks, to review your sessions. Do this outside your normal half-hour session. It takes approximately an hour to review a week of sessions. Reading them over can deepen your insight on the progress you have made during the last several weeks. List the days you are reviewing and make comments on each. Here is what a week's review might look like:

April 2: Mostly question and answer, talked about Lisa and work problems.

April 3: Self-esteem session. My Inner Child was resistant but enjoyed the session. Inner Child wanted to go to the park for a picnic lunch.

April 4: Self-esteem session. Worked on confidence, organization and happiness.

April 5: Inner Conflict. Couldn't decide whether to buy a new car or fix the old one. Decided to price some new cars and get new shocks for now.

April 6: Goal-setting session. Worked on what I want to do during the next six months to learn more graphics skills.

April 7: Question-and-answer session. Went over general stuff.

April 8: Love, support and nurture: Lost job. Inner Child was upset about what happened at work on Friday. Inner Parent was afraid it couldn't get another job.

Your descriptions can be as short or detailed as you like. You can study your pattern of progress practicing Self-Parenting without contacting or working directly with the Inner Child. Keep these review sessions in your binder after the sections you have reviewed, or create a separate section for them in your session binder. You will also find that you jog your memory on plans or ideas you may have forgotten.

Outside Your Sessions

As an intermediate practitioner of the SELF-PARENTING Program, you will soon be looking for ways to increase your Self-Parenting awareness outside your sessions. Some methods are:

- Do something nice once a day for your Inner Child in the "real world," something you would not ordinarily do.
- Compliment your Inner Child out loud after a job well done, such as making a difficult parking space on the first try or completing a difficult phone call.
- Consult your Inner Child specifically before any purchasing decisions.
- Pay close attention to your Inner Child's opinion, especially in a pressure situation.

Other suggestions:

- Have a beautiful room or spot in your home for your Inner Child.
- Read a bedtime story to your Inner Child.
- Go to a playground. Ride on the swings or play in a sand box.
- Go to the circus or the zoo.
- Visit a pet store.
- Take a train ride.
- Go on a picnic or to the beach with your Inner Child.
- Build something with wooden blocks.
- Visit a toy store and pick out something special your Inner Child likes.

Inner Child Complaining "Past The Point"

There may come a time when your Inner Child complains or criticizes you, as the Inner Parent, past the point of reason. It makes statements such as, "You don't love me," or "You don't care about me." When you ask your Inner Child why it feels that way, it doesn't give you any specific reason but continues to complain.

At some point you might have to lay down the law. You may need to let your Inner Child know that the time for complaining and griping is over. If you are certain that you are loving, supporting and nurturing your child in obvious ways (such as consistent half-hour sessions for several months) and your Inner Child has no specific complaints that you are not acting on, you may be ready for this step.

At some point in your sessions, especially if you have been a weak Inner Parent in the past, you may just have to let your Inner Child know that you are back and in charge. The easiest way to do this is to point out to your Inner Child that you have been practicing positive Self-Parenting for several months and show your Inner Child the proof.

You can also ask your Inner Child this question:

"Inner Child, how many other Inner Parents have been doing half-hour sessions with their Inner Child for _____ months?"

With this question you are suggesting that your Inner Child recognize that you are doing the best you can as the Inner Parent, that you will continue to do so and you just don't need constant complaining if there is nothing specific to complain about. Perhaps vague complaints were acceptable several months ago but now they are not, and you can quietly and directly let your Inner Child know this.

What is happening is your Inner Child is continuing to base its complaints on the "old" Inner Parent rather than the "new" Inner Parent. Usually a word to the wise will resolve this type of situation along with the physical evidence of commitment (a growing stack of half-hour sessions) to back you up.

Ways to Respond to Your Inner Child Outside Your Sessions

You are protected from roadblocking your Inner Child during your sessions by following the session format. But you are becoming much more aware of the desires and needs of your Inner Child outside your sessions. What happens if your Inner Child, in one of its many ways, becomes emotional or reactive during the day?

There is a simple but effective response you can make as the Inner Parent. In fact, it is the identical response that you use during your sessions. If your

Inner Child is emotional or complains during the day, just acknowledge it by saying,

> "Thank you, Inner Child, for telling me that."

Under most circumstances, just letting your Inner Child release its emotions, with no response other than listening and thanking it, is like letting steam escape from your radiator. Nothing else needs to be done. Just let the steam escape and continue with your life. You will usually have your best results by listening only and not responding to your Inner Child with additional dialogue. If a problem persists, you can work the Eight Steps of Inner Conflict Resolution.

If your Inner Child screams for attention or becomes extremely emotional when you have something else to do, you can say out loud to your Inner Child something like:

> "Inner Child, I know you want to tell me everything right now and I know it is quite important for you, but please tell me during our next half-hour session, not now. Right now we have got to get on with our outer life. Please tell me tomorrow everything you are telling me today."

Keep Up Your Reading

The Inner Parent must continue to read and educate itself on positive Self-Parenting and communication skills. Unfortunately, this is not a subject we are taught in school. It takes repetition and continuous study to learn how to pay attention and respond appropriately to your Inner Child outside of your sessions. The book *Parent Effectiveness Training (P.E.T.)*, by Thomas Gordon, is a very effective tool to educate your Inner Parent during your second three months of Self-Parenting. Until you have read *P.E.T.*, you will not understand how much trouble you can get into. Every page of *P.E.T.* contains practical insights for practitioners of Self-Parenting.

As you deepen your understanding and practice of Self-Parenting, you will find there are many sources of information that can help you improve your

Self-Parenting style. When you read a magazine article about the boss/ employee relationship at work, you might see a parallel to your Inner Parent. Your neighbor could tell you a story about her friend that relates directly to your Inner Child.

There are many opportunities and ways the Inner Parent can advance its education. The key is to keep an open mind and be seeking ways to improve your Self-Parenting style. Depending on your level of skill and your determination, you will eventually create your own style of positive Self-Parenting. When you can apply these and other intermediate communication skills within your Inner Conversations, you will be well rewarded.

THE WEAK INNER PARENT

Two more diagnostic categories are useful when discussing problems with Self-Parenting: the strong Inner Parent and the weak Inner Parent.

The Strong Inner Parent

The strong Inner Parent takes an active, assertive role in its Self-Parenting style. This Inner Parent is happy to be the director and the boss. It is definitely running the show whether the Inner Child is on board or not. When the strong Inner Parent is negative, it creates active grief for the Inner Child in many ways, usually through abuse such as blaming, ridiculing or being authoritarian. These are the typical patterns of behavior that roadblock the Inner Child. When the strong Inner Parent is positive, it can move mountains and accomplish miracles in support of its Inner Child. It uses every means available to love, support and nurture the Inner Child to the best of its ability.

The strong Inner Parent with a negative Self-Parenting style can make a dramatic recovery practicing the SELF-PARENTING Program. Because of its innate strength, the strong Inner Parent has the power to stop abusing its Inner Child almost immediately, which creates a positive sense of relief. Secondly, when the strong Inner Parent begins changing from a negative to a positive Self-Parenting style, its strength becomes an asset rather than a liability.

The Weak Inner Parent

The weak Inner Parent is the opposite of the strong Inner Parent. Most problems in your Self-Parenting style are the result of a weak Inner Parent.

If you have this problem, it may take many half-hour sessions before you become aware of this condition. For example, in the early days of sessions it is quite common for weak Inner Parents to try "being a friend" to their Inner Child. If the Inner Child gives them strong emotional negativity during their session, they try to pacify or relieve the Inner Child's emotion. In the guise of nurturing their Inner Child, they wind up roadblocking or abusing it.

As a weak Inner Parent you may be trapped in a rut, unable to take the steps it is increasingly clear you should take. As your Self-Parenting sessions accumulate, you will experience more and more aspects of your negative Self-Parenting style first-hand. At first you will think this is because you have such a bad Inner Child. Eventually, you will find these negative experiences are caused by your Inner Parent.

A typical problem for the weak Inner Parent is one of attitude. The people who say "I don't have the time," have Inner Parents who are unwilling to take responsibility for their Inner Child. They use excuses to defend the weak ways of their Inner Parent. They complain that the SELF-PARENTING Program is "too structured" and "takes so much time and energy" or that "my Inner Child doesn't like it." This is a key indicator that the Inner Parent is speaking, because the Inner Child *ALWAYS* appreciates sessions. Often when the person finally does begin practicing sessions, the Inner Child lets loose with a blast of pent-up emotions that have been suppressed for years. This tends to frighten the weak Inner Parent, who becomes scared and wants to stop doing the sessions.

The weak Inner Parent is prone to neglecting the Inner Child. It doesn't take responsibility for any of the actions it should. This Inner Parent doesn't keep deadlines, doesn't pay attention to the Inner Child and ignores the advice or pleas of the Inner Child.

A weak Inner Parent follows a program of inaction or passive allowance, drifting wherever life takes it. Of course, this weakness of personality affects the lives of both Inner Selves. Often the Inner Child attempts to take over for the weak Inner Parent and run the show. The Inner Child may be in control, but unfortunately this arrangement can't work.

The weak Inner Parent does not do what it's supposed to do. It is not fulfilling its role within the Inner Conversations. It is passive, neglectful and unresponsive to the needs of the Inner Child. Achieving a positive Self-Parenting style is going to be a battle for the weak Inner Parent. Reversing a long-standing trend as a weak Inner Parent is not an easy process. Recovery is usually a series of wins and losses as the Inner Parent struggles to regain its rightful role in Self-Parenting.

Another major problem with the weak Inner Parent is that the Inner Child is continually forced to tell the weak Inner Parent what to do and how to do it. This type of advice sounds so much like a parent that the Inner Parent wonders which self is which and becomes even more confused and unsure.

The SELF-PARENTING Program has defined four classic weaknesses of the Inner Parent. The weak Inner Parent is usually practicing one or more of these behaviors. If you are experiencing trouble with your Self-Parenting style, consider these four classic weaknesses associated with the weak or negative Inner Parent:

- Avoiding responsibility for its role within the Inner Conversations
- Failing to problem-solve Inner Conflicts with a Win/Win solution
- Neglecting the feelings or viewpoints of the Inner Child
- Abusing the Inner Child with negative Self-Parenting

Naturally, the objective of positive Self-Parenting is for the Inner Parent to change its classic weaknesses into classic strengths.

Classic Weakness No. 1: Avoiding responsibility for its role in the Inner Conversations

One of the things negative Inner Parents do best is to avoid or deny responsibility for the realities in their lives. They often attempt to put the blame for their lives' conditions on other people or outer circumstances. Their reasoning is that if they don't accept responsibility, they don't have to accept the blame. Unfortunately, this is not the truth of the situation.

Within your Inner Conversations, the Inner Parent is completely responsible for the effects and conditions of your life. The weak Inner Parent tries to deny this and gives many rationales as to why everything wrong in life is not its fault. The only problem is that none of these excuses apply. The Inner Parent is solely responsible for the overall condition of your Inner Conversations.

Classic Weakness No. 2: Failing to problem-solve Inner Conflicts with a Win/Win solution

It is up to the Inner Parent to problem-solve any Inner Conflicts that might come up. The Inner Child can't do it because it doesn't have the leadership position. People in the outside world can't do it because they can't hear the Inner Conflict inside your mind. For these reasons your Inner Parent is responsible for:

1. Recognizing the presence of an Inner Conflict
2. Writing out the Inner Conversation
3. Successfully resolving the conflict of needs between the Inner Parent and Inner Child in a Win/Win manner

The weak Inner Parent does not follow this prescription. Most of the time the unaware or untrained Inner Parent uses the Win/Lose method to resolve Inner Conflicts. This works out wonderfully for the temporary needs of the Inner Parent, but of course it is bad news for the Inner Child. Occasionally a strong-willed Inner Child will create a Lose/Win or Lose/Lose resolution to strike back. In this circumstance the Inner Parent loses its ability to control the Inner Child, who therefore achieves a temporary "win" to the detriment of the Inner Parent. Yet all three of these problem-solving methods are unsatisfactory for the optimal functioning of both selves. The Win/Win resolution is the only acceptable solution for an Inner Conflict.

Classic Weakness No. 3: Neglecting the feelings or viewpoints of the Inner Child

Neglect covers the passive behaviors of the weak Inner Parent such as inattention, overlooking, forgetting or abandonment. In these circumstances, it is not abuse by the Inner Parent that hurts the Inner Child. It is the lack of attention or appropriate response to the voice inside. A plant needs water, food and light. If you neglect the plant, it will die. If your Inner Parent neglects your Inner Child, you will experience many negative emotional effects.

The Inner Child has feelings and emotions. Since it is a separate self from you as the Inner Parent, you do not have the right to negate or deny those feelings. Failure to acknowledge and accept the feelings of your Inner Child denies one half of you. Denial of any one type of feeling will cause you to suppress the full range of feelings. This requires so much energy and/or attention by the Inner Parent that it can immobilize your Inner Conversations completely, bringing them to a standstill.

Some people say, "Well, I only deny the negative feelings. I always accept the positive feelings." Unfortunately, it is not possible to repress only bad feelings and accept only good feelings. Feelings (your Inner Child) do not work this way. A well-known psychological principle states that if you try to deny your negative feelings, then you must necessarily deny your positive feelings as well. Negative and positive feelings are two sides of the same "feeling" coin.

Many times this denial is simply the lack of awareness. Before Self-Parenting concepts became known, Inner Conversations were not recognized or specifically addressed in a practical way. The average person was not aware of having a constant inner dialogue and most certainly did not know who the specific voices were having these conversations. Many people were afraid even to mention this internal dialogue for fear that others might think them "crazy" or "schizophrenic."

Classic Weakness No. 4: Abusing the Inner Child with negative Self-Parenting

This problem is much more widespread than is generally known. You learn by observation from an early age how to become an Inner Parent to your Inner Child. If that upbringing was negative or abusive, you will do the "normal" thing, which is to treat your Inner Child the same way you were treated. Unfortunately this behavior can equate to Inner Child abuse. Unknowingly, you can do terrible things to your Inner Child within your Inner

Conversations. A constant stream of criticism and negativity can cause your Inner Child to experience a severe state of unhappiness or depression.

The weak Inner Parent often describes his or her attempts to become a positive Inner Parent as a struggle or a battle. Unfortunately, there is no one else to do this work except the Inner Parent. Receiving outside help may provide a temporary transition, but it is merely a postponement of the inevitable. For lasting change to occur, the Inner Parent must take responsibility.

The weak Inner Parent is the one who derives the most benefit from the SELF-PARENTING Support Groups. These groups provide the most effective ally the Inner Parent can have in its struggle. Members can help each other sustain their Inner Parents' motivation to change its Self-Parenting style by reinforcing its efforts and providing a forum to learn more about positive Self-Parenting. If you have any of the four classic signs of a weak Inner Parent, the closest SELF-PARENTING Support Group is where you want to be. The group will help you by supporting your weak Inner Parent until you can gain enough experience to be strong on your own.

THE NEUROLOGICAL BASIS
OF SELF-PARENTING

The psychological concept of Self-Parenting has a solid basis in brain anatomy and physiology. In the future, when the dual disciplines of brain neurology and computer programming have advanced far beyond what we know today, researchers will be able to attach electrodes to the left and right sides of the brain to gather a printout of a person's Inner Conversations. They will then be able to correlate these findings with the sociological make-up and background of the subject's parents and probably trace the person's Self-Parenting style back a few generations.

Although the unbiased and scientific verification of the physiological basis of Self-Parenting may be a long time coming, for now we can consider some interesting facts that are well known in scientific circles. Perhaps this line of inquiry will become the focus for research in the future. The rationale is present today. What we need now are some solid investigative data.

The human brain is a dual organ. It actually consists of two separate halves, each capable of advanced, although separate, functions. Each half of the brain has a different way of processing information. The left brain uses words, the right brain uses sensory images. Thinking is associated with the left brain (the Inner Parent) and feeling is associated with the right brain (the Inner Child). By seeing how the two brains function individually, you can see the basis for the two sides of your Inner Conversations, the Inner Parent and the Inner Child.

Here is a compilation of the different functional modes of the left and right brains:

Left Brain (Inner Parent)   Right Brain (Inner Child)

Left Brain (Inner Parent)	Right Brain (Inner Child)
Logical thinking	Emotional feeling
Talker	Doer
Thinker	Dreamer
Very wordy	Non-verbal
Verbal memory	Visual memory
Uses logic	Uses intuition
Writing	Recognizing visual patterns
Formulation of ideas	Interpreting sensations
Complex math	Music appreciation
Reason	Passion, instinct
Conscious	Unconscious
Affected	Natural
Rational	Mysterious
Singing lyrics	Humming tunes
Reading	Watching television or movies
Looks at details	Sees the overall picture
Linear deductions	Hunches, "vibes"
Language skills	Visual or spatial skills
Achievement of specific goal	Sensation of the activity
Speech, speaking	Musical discrimination and pitch

The brain's optimum functioning occurs when the two halves of the brain act as partners. In other words, the thinking brain and the feeling brain need to develop a working relationship. They do this by communicating along a neural pathway linking the two brains. This bundle of nerve fibers, about the thickness of a pencil, is called the *corpus callosum.* This is the *ONLY* connection between the two hemispheres. Without the corpus callosum, the human brain would indeed function as two separate organs.

As a means of studying brain physiology and function, researchers from various disciplines have examined what they call "split-brain" patients. These are patients who have had their corpus callosum severed for medical reasons. By conducting physiological and psychological tests on these patients, scientists have discovered much about the function of the two sides of the brain.

For example, it has been shown in split-brain patients that the right hemisphere (the Inner Child) can generate completely independent emotional reactions which the left brain (Inner Parent) is unable to explain verbally.

Part of the brain's function is to create the experience of self-awareness or conscious interaction between these two distinctly different selves or personalities. One side is a rational, thinking, logical self represented by the research associated with the left brain — the Inner Parent. The other is an emotional, feeling, intuitive self identified with the right brain — the Inner Child.

As an infant, each person has an "open architecture" that is programmed by outer parents or adult caretakers. The left and right brains interpret life experiences according to their respective anatomical frames of reference. The two brains are biologically ordained to absorb and mimic the behavior of the humans around them to develop and establish their own function. Thus, each child absorbs and eventually begins to reflect the feelings, attitudes and values of its parents, relatives and social environment.

By the age of seven the physical brain and nervous system are largely complete and the size of an adult's. Your neural network has internalized a vast set of "operating instructions" which you then use to assume your role in society. Your experience of Self-Parenting is the natural effect of the neurological functioning of your brain. Consequently, you are Self-Parenting with the Self-Parenting style you were given without having any conscious choice in the way you were programmed. Trying to stop your Self-Parenting would be like trying to stop your breathing or the beating of your heart. Only as an adult, can you begin choosing the way you want to parent yourself in a conscious manner.

To sum up the scientific rationale behind Self-Parenting: Self-Parenting is the condition of interaction between your left brain (the Inner Parent) and your right brain (the Inner Child) along a nerve pathway called the corpus callosum. Your awareness is created by the conscious attention you maintain of the communication between the left brain (your Inner Parent) and right brain (your Inner Child) inside your mind (your Inner Conversations).

SELF-PARENTING AND THE MEDIA

The media interest anyone who is an observer of the human condition. The SELF-PARENTING Program maintains an interest in the media since they reflect the Inner Conversations of their audience. The most popular media presentations are those that reflect most clearly the inner thoughts and feelings of the greatest number of people. In other words, the most popular movies, television shows and songs are the ones that best reflect our Inner Conversations back to us. When we feel or experience our inner reality as a result of viewing or listening to external media, we are entertained. We are affected by the media in spite of ourselves.

The classics become classics because they so perfectly represent the Inner Conversations within us. They go beyond the fad or style of a certain year or decade to the universal human experience. The better the particular medium can do this, the more popular it is. Witness the universal appeal of movies such as *The Wizard of Oz* or *The Sound of Music,* or songs such as "My Way," which will always be relevant to the human experience. They contain principles or situations that reflect and always will reflect the dynamics of human Inner Conversations.

Television

Most television stifles the imagination. If you have been brought up on a diet of 30 or more hours a week of television, your imagination (i.e., your Inner Child) will be emotionally flat. For many people, television-watching is a serious impediment to their Self-Parenting progress.

Television has a hypnotic effect on your Inner Child. If the Inner Parent is not discriminating, the Inner Child will watch whatever is on television just because the screen is flickering and sound is coming out of the box. People often use television as a way of tuning out their Inner Conversations. They turn on their television to turn off what they are thinking and feeling.

Some people say they can't find time to do half-hour sessions. Are they spending three hours a night watching television? Do they flip on the TV the minute they wake up in the morning "just for company?" These people would be better off sharing their morning with their Inner Child through a half-hour session.

If you would like to experience your Inner Conversations in a deeper way, stop all television cold turkey for a month. Not everyone will want or need to do this, of course, but those who do will experience a plethora of benefits. Typically, the ones who need it most will be the ones least likely to do it. For some this will be the best way to cut through the mental fog shrouding the awareness of their Inner Conversations.

"TV numbing," as one practitioner called it, should especially be avoided when your Inner Conversations are particularly emotional. As the Inner Parent, you must be aware if you or your Inner Child are using television to numb your Inner Conversations. If you find yourself overdosing, take positive action just as an outer parent might do when confronted with a similar situation.

However, television can also be used as a learning tool by the Inner Parent. Many programs can educate and entertain your Inner Child in a positive manner. It is part of your Inner Parent's responsibility to manage the television diet of your Inner Child so that too many empty emotional calories will not leave it starving emotionally.

Music

Music has a profound effect on the Inner Child. In fact, many people habitually replace the natural emotions and feelings of their Inner Child (which may be negative) with artificial emotions induced by music. This technique has recently become a commercial bonanza, with ad agencies using popular music standards from the '60s, to pitch their '90s consumable products. It is really quite ingenious.

The '60s kids represent the largest consumer generation (the baby boomers), and they love their music. Ad agencies take a popular song from that time that instantly creates a positive emotional response within the Inner Child of a '60s kid. They then associate this positive emotion with their product. This technique manipulates the Inner Child very powerfully and is so successful that it has been copied in almost every product category.

Music is also used by people as a substitute for listening to their Inner Conversations, especially in their cars. Any kind of music, even classical or New Age music, can numb your awareness to what is going on inside your mind. Music creates its own emotional stimuli, which prevent you from being attuned to your own internal feelings. The external source of power drowns out or replaces the inner awareness of your thoughts and feelings.

If you *ALWAYS* listen to music in your car, try not playing any and listening to your Inner Conversations instead. You may be surprised at what you hear.

Advertising and Your Inner Child

The Inner Child is the self most susceptible to emotional and subconscious programming such as that used in television advertising. ("Two all-beef patties, special sauce, lettuce, cheese, pickles, onions, on a . . . .") Your Inner Child is the self the advertisers are trying to reach. They are much less interested in your Inner Parent. They know that if they can generate a strong emotional response within your Inner Child and associate it with their product, your Inner Parent will be happy to buy their brand of soap without rational inquiry. Have you ever noticed how children watching television are often more captivated by the commercials than the shows themselves?

The Inner Parent can analyze why this and that is not true, doesn't work or why a commercial is completely false. But none of that matters. Ad agencies and advertisers know from the millions of dollars of research they conduct each year how to generate a strong emotional response from your Inner Child and associate this desired feeling with their product. They know they are likely to get a purchase response from you even if it is several years from now. They have exhaustive profiles on the wants and needs of your Inner Child, although they are not using these terms. When you go to the store and see their product, they make sure your Inner Child subconsciously remembers their ad and influences your Inner Parent (during an Inner Conversation) to buy that product. You, as the Inner Parent, will most likely be oblivious to this process.

Media Over-Stimulation

The loss of one's inner sense of self (ego strength) due to the lack of bonding between the Inner Parent and Inner Child is accompanied by a corresponding demand for outer stimulation. This lack of an "inner core" creates a feeling of emptiness inside. The resultant rush to fill this inner emptiness with outer stimulation is very prevalent in modern society.

How many times have you been sitting at a stoplight when a driver pulling up next to you has music on so loud it hurts *your* ears? What is that person doing? They are drowning out the empty cry of their Inner Conversations. They are replacing the calling out for attention by their Inner Child with the artificial emotions stimulated by the music. Lacking intimacy with their Inner Child, such people create false intimacy by manipulating and pumping their Inner Conversations with outer stimuli.

If you put the average person in an isolation cell with no television or music, he or she would be disoriented for days until the natural flow of the Inner Conversations became reestablished. Modern media create and sustain the average person's sense of reality from the outside, rather than enabling each person to think and feel for themselves. In today's world, even Thoreau might be out at the Walden Pond shopping mall picnic area with his CD deck and a video player, sipping soft drinks.

Toxic Parent Show

There was a recent talk show on "toxic parenting." The guest, a therapist, was insisting that a young woman who had received dysfunctional parenting "get in touch with her 'real' feelings" about how she felt when she received negative parenting from her father. By Self-Parenting standards this is completely the wrong approach.

A person with a legacy of toxic parenting is going to have a legacy of toxic Self-Parenting. Getting in touch with her "real" feelings about how she was parented is not only a waste of time, it is counterproductive. Her emotions and feelings are the *RESULT* of the abuse and neglect that dysfunctional parenting gave her as a child, not the *CAUSE* of her problems.

The advice she was getting from the therapist was like telling a person who is starving that the cure for hunger is experiencing, getting in touch with and really *"FEELING"* the hunger. What good is that going to do? A person who is starving doesn't need to feel more hunger. *A PERSON WHO IS STARVING NEEDS FOOD.*

What this young lady who had received toxic parenting needs to do as an Inner Parent is to quit concentrating on her past experiences and begin to love, support and nurture her Inner Child in a direct and physical way now. This practice will create and establish new feelings of love, happiness and joy which will cause her Inner Child to begin feeling loved. This will be like giving food to a starving person, not wasting time having them getting in touch with their hunger.

As long as therapists keep insisting that their clients "get in touch" with their negative feelings, people will continue to recreate and restimulate the forgotten, negative emotions that are the effect, not the cause, of their problem. The methods of the SELF-PARENTING Program have started to reverse this trend in a small way so that now people can be spared this abusive process.

Getting in touch with the remnant feelings of anger that resulted from neglect or abuse is counter-productive to the healing process. Anger and other negative emotions are secondary effects to the frustration of not receiving love. The way to heal a childhood of abuse and neglect from dysfunctional parenting is to love, support and nurture your Inner Child right now, today. The greater the level of awareness by the Inner Parent in this regard, the greater the happiness and support (healing) of the Inner Child.

6

DETERMINING YOUR INNER CHILD'S NEEDS

The Problem

Most people are not in touch with the needs of their Inner Child. For them, trying to pinpoint their Inner Child's needs is like searching for a needle in a haystack. The needs of the Inner Child appear too complex to sort out without a simple method. This leaves the Inner Child frustrated because its needs aren't being met. The Inner Parent is also frustrated since it wants to support the Inner Child but doesn't know how to determine the specific area in which to work.

The Solution

The Inner Parent can learn a special technique to determine the Inner Child's needs. Learning to classify needs into four basic categories — physical, emotional, mental and social — gives the Inner Parent a specific way to interpret and monitor vague requests by the Inner Child. Each need category can be quickly scanned by the Inner Parent to identify the specific one. This process is called "Thinking Needs."

INTRODUCTION TO YOUR INNER CHILD'S NEEDS

An interesting way to begin the study of needs is to examine the relationship with your Inner Child from another perspective. We have established that all people are having Inner Conversations within their minds. You also know that your Inner Parent parents your Inner Child with a Self-Parenting style that may be positive or negative. This understanding comes from looking at Self-Parenting from the Inner Parent's perspective. But what would happen if we asked the following two-part question:

Why would an Inner Child want to communicate with an Inner Parent?

What motivates the Inner Child to speak to the Inner Parent in the first place?

If you try to answer this question before reading on, you will find it difficult. This question and its resulting answer have given the SELF-PARENTING Program a unique insight into the relationship between the two Inner Selves. The answer to this question provides the path to a much deeper understanding of the daily interaction you experience with your Inner Child.

Think about this for a moment. Why would an Inner Child want to communicate with an Inner Parent? What causes the Inner Child to initiate conversation with the Inner Parent in the first place? When the Inner Child is reaching out to the Inner Parent, what is it trying to accomplish?

The SELF-PARENTING Program has established three possible reasons why the Inner Child initiates communication with the Inner Parent. Understanding these motivations will help you to know your Inner Child more deeply.

The reasons your Inner Child initiates communication are:
1. Your Inner Child wants to share an observation or express a viewpoint.
2. Your Inner Child has a question or a request for information.
3. Your Inner Child is asking for a need to be met.

Fortunately, you have already begun the process of paying conscious attention to your Inner Child. Your next step, responding appropriately, requires you to interpret *WHY* your Inner Child is communicating. Naturally, you must be aware enough to identify your Inner Child's voice within your Inner Conversations. Usually this ability comes with three to six months of half-hour sessions. This gives you enough time to practice listening to your Inner Conversations as well as to experience the interaction between the two inner voices.

Most people have trouble maintaining a sense of contact with their Inner Child during day-to-day activities in the "real world." It takes many months of half-hour sessions before you can develop the conscious awareness that is required. Even if you can hear what your Inner Child is saying, it is still a challenge to interpret its communications correctly.

Unfortunately, the skills of paying attention and responding appropriately to your Inner Child are not taught in school. Without a simple and effective procedure to follow, you will find it difficult to understand what your Inner Child is "really" saying. Your Inner Parent must practice to correctly interpret the vague messages of your Inner Child.

Another major complication is that your Inner Child doesn't know how to communicate clearly. Much as a two-year-old knows exactly what it wants but can't express it clearly in words, your Inner Child knows exactly what it wants but may have trouble communicating it to you. Your Inner Child has learned a variety of communication methods to express itself, some of them positive and some not. It's up to the Inner Parent to learn to "translate" these communications and respond to them appropriately.

In order to determine the underlying purpose of your Inner Child's communications, you will ask yourself three simple questions as the Inner Parent.

Each question helps you to examine your Inner Child's communication. By asking each question in order, you will find it easier to determine the purpose behind your Inner Child's message.

As an added bonus, each question also eliminates a confusing array of options that do not apply to your Inner Child's statements. This is the secret to this method and the reason it is so effective.

Special Note: People often suggest that "spiritual needs" are being left out as part of this process. The SELF-PARENTING Program does not include "spiritual needs" as part of this evaluation for the following reasons:

The relationship between the Inner Parent and Inner Child is fully based on the physical, emotional, mental and social realities of the "real world." Many people, especially those with a weak Inner Parent, try to seek a "spiritual" solution to a problem that is really based on a physical, emotional, mental or social need. Seeking a "spiritual" solution in this case is simply another form of denial or avoidance of the Inner Child's needs by a negative Inner Parent. The solution to your problems with your Inner Child will always be found in one of the four basic needs categories.

Another factor is that each person has a different definition of spiritual while most people agree on the definition of the term social. In fact, if you look at social interaction carefully, you will find that positive social behavior meets a definition that most people consider "spiritual" whereas negative social behavior would be described by most people as "not spiritual." Until a person is able to correctly define and discuss the physical, emotional, mental and social needs categories, he or she will be unable to recognize or comprehend spiritual needs.

HOW TO "THINK NEEDS"

This section describes the exact technique of interpreting your Inner Child's communication to you, the Inner Parent. Although each step is spelled out for clarity, the actual process often takes only a few seconds.

When your Inner Child communicates to you, ask yourself the following three questions:
1. Is my Inner Child sharing?
2. Is my Inner Child requesting information?
3. Is my Inner Child expressing a need?

1. Is My Inner Child Sharing?

This is usually very easy to determine. When your Inner Child communicates on this level it is simply expressing its mood or sharing an opinion from its side of the Inner Conversations. Usually, these are light disclosures that arise from your Inner Child's appreciation or observation of life. Often it is telling you something it thinks you ought to know.

> *"Wow, what a beautiful day!"*
> *"Is it hot, or what?"*
> *"That was a stupid thing for that lady to do."*
> *"That teacher was so kind to us."*
> *"I think we should leave soon, before it starts to rain."*

These messages can be quite casual and conversational in nature, like speaking with friends or even a stranger on the street. Whether an offhand mention, a frivolous thought or a muddled impression, your Inner Child is simply sharing part of itself with you.

Another possibility is that your Inner Child may be trying to help you or give advice. This type of communication can take many forms but it is usually a warning via a pointed statement.

> *"Watch out for that guy, I don't trust him."*
> *"I hear a truck with screeching brakes about 20 feet behind us."*
> *"The last time we drove home that late we were stuck in traffic for an hour."*
> *"This contract is too important not to take to a lawyer."*
> *"Maybe we'd better wait a few days."*

When the Inner Child is communicating on this level, it often has the Inner Parent's best interest at heart and is offering insightful advice that is intuitive in nature. You are being given a warning that there might be something to do or watch out for in the future. This is a particularly good time to be paying attention to your Inner Child.

When your Inner Child is sharing, just by listening and accepting what it says, you are responding appropriately. If you roadblock your Inner Child or try to change or deny what your Inner Child is saying or feeling, then you are responding negatively. Practicing sessions for a few months should give you the skills to respond appropriately as an Inner Parent in this situation.

2. Is My Inner Child Requesting Information?

If your Inner Child is requesting some information, then you have a job to do if you want to respond appropriately. You must find out the information that the Inner Child wants to know.

Many times the Inner Child simply wants some clarification of what you said as the Inner Parent. Or it may have some questions about an upcoming situation such as a job interview or a cross-country move. Your Inner Child might want you to look up scholarship opportunities, classes in acting or how much it costs to fly to Vancouver. It could ask you hundreds of questions during the day, just like an outer child might.

Whatever information your Inner Child would like to know, the role of the Inner Parent is to find out and relay the info back to the Inner Child. Just as the positive outer parent patiently answers the outer child's questions, the Inner Parent should do the same for the Inner Child.

If your Inner Child makes such a request during your session, you should write it down on your "To Do" list. If this request for information comes during your daily activities, it will be much harder to recognize.

This is one area where many Inner Parents are weak. Either they are not paying enough attention to even hear the question, or they respond inappropriately by not answering or forgetting that the Inner Child even asked the question. This is one important area where your responsibilities as an Inner Parent will be put to the test.

3. Is My Inner Child Expressing a Need?

If your Inner Child is asking for a need to be met, then the Inner Parent must become a detective. Determining the specific purpose behind your Inner Child's communication can be a challenge for the Inner Parent. For example, it is very rare for your Inner Child to say, "Hello, Inner Parent, are you listening? I have a need and my need is _____."

You will often be required to interpret a statement that doesn't make sense at all, given your current circumstances. Only after asking your Inner Child for clarification does the meaning of its statement become clear. Sometimes you have to be pretty sharp as an Inner Parent to interpret the underlying need based on what your Inner Child actually says. In order to respond appropriately, you will have to evaluate the exact nature of your Inner Child's need using the "Thinking Needs" process.

Here is the key concept to understand for interpreting a *yes* answer to the third question:

IF YOUR INNER CHILD IS NOT SHARING OR ASKING FOR INFORMA-
TION, IT IS ASKING FOR A NEED TO BE MET.

What you must do next as an Inner Parent is to determine exactly what type of need your Inner Child is expressing. Here is a further clarification of this third purpose behind your Inner Child's desire to communicate.

You already know your Inner Child has a need because of the *no* answer to the first two questions. Now you must determine what kind of need your Inner Child has. You accomplish this by asking two more questions. The first question asks your Inner Child to specify a general need category. The second question will help your Inner Child tell you exactly what need it has.

Be clear on this point. You are still *ASKING* your Inner Child what need it has, not *TELLING* it what you think. As the Inner Parent you are requesting clarification from your Inner Child, not ordering it how to feel. You are helping your Inner Child by giving it a selection of choices, rather than forcing it to come up with an answer on its own. Until your Inner Child informs you of a specific need, you are still in the "paying attention" phase of being a positive Inner Parent.

Once you have determined that your Inner Child is asking for a need to be met, your next question to the Inner Child is:

"Inner Child, do you have a physical, emotional, mental or social need?"

This question allows your Inner Child the opportunity to narrow down what it wants into one of four categories. Let your Inner Child think about this for a few seconds while waiting patiently for an answer. Your Inner Child will then generally tell you one of these four choices.

Once it tells you the general category, you will have to clarify the specific type of physical, emotional, mental or social need your Inner Child has. You do this by asking this next question:

"Inner Child, what is your (physical [or whichever choice]) need?"

Placing your Inner Child's first answer into the second question helps your Inner Child to clarify what it wants.

"REAL WORLD" EXAMPLES OF "THINKING NEEDS"

Here is an example of how this might work. You are walking along the street and inside your mind you hear your Inner Child make one of the following statements:

> *"Let's go across the street."*
> *"When are we going to get home?"*
> *"Why didn't you bring any money?"*

Since you are paying attention and heard what your Inner Child said, you ask yourself mentally, "Is my Inner Child sharing an observation or asking for some specific information?"

Even though your Inner Child is making a suggestion with the first statement and seems to be asking for information in the next two statements, the context in which these comments are made simply doesn't make sense to you as the Inner Parent. These statements seem to be made with enough energy to make you wonder, "What is my Inner Child saying?" or "Why does my Inner Child want to cross the street right now?" This leaves you with a *yes* answer to the third possibility, "Is my Inner Child expressing a need?"

Now that you suspect your Inner Child is asking for a need to be met, you must clarify what it is. Based on what it has told you so far, you just can't tell. Your next step is to ask mentally:

"Inner Child, do you have a physical, emotional, mental or social need?"

The beauty of this question is that it is still an open-ended question. Your Inner Child is being asked if there is a deeper level to what it is saying. After a second or two of consideration, your Inner Child says, "Yes, I have a physical need." Now your final step is to ask,

"Inner Child, what is your (physical) need?"

In this situation, your Inner Child tells you it is hungry and it wants some food. Now you have a specific idea of the purpose behind your Inner Child's communication.

As you can see, there was no way you could tell your Inner Child was hungry based on:

> *"Let's go across the street."*
> *"When are we going to get home?"*
> *"Why didn't you bring any money?"*

These comments were simply too obscure. Because you were paying attention to what your Inner Child was saying, you asked for clarification. You were then able to determine that it had a need, so you simply directed your questions in the above manner. This invited and allowed your Inner Child, in a positive and supportive way, to give you more specific input.

A More Complex Example of "Thinking Needs"

Here is another example using a more difficult set of statements. Suppose your Inner Child tells you any one of following:

> *"I want to take a course in acting."*
> *"We need to take a course in acting."*
> *"How come we can't act?"*
> *"You never do anything for me."*

With each of these statements the Inner Child is expressing a need to take an acting course. The first two statements would be easy to evaluate if the Inner Parent was paying attention. The third statement would be trickier to interpret even if the Inner Parent was paying attention. The fourth statement would create problems. Here is a situation when you want to ask your Inner Child to clarify why it was making this particular statement.

You would begin when you heard your Inner Child say:

"You never do anything for me."

As the Inner Parent you might sense that this message is deeper than simple sharing or asking for information. Even though the statement could be interpreted as sharing ("You never do anything for me"), this is not specific enough to reveal what your Inner Child truly wants. Therefore your reaction would be to think, "My Inner Child isn't making any sense. I wonder what it is really asking for?"

To clarify what your Inner Child wants, start on square one with the question:

"Inner Child, do you have a physical, emotional, mental or social need?"

After waiting a bit your Inner Child says, "Emotional." Next you ask:

"Inner Child, what is your (emotional) need?"

As a result, your Inner Child tells you it wants to take an acting class so it can become famous. Instead of wondering why your Inner Child is being negative with you for days, you can now discover what it wants in seconds.

"Thinking Needs" is an extremely powerful process for the aware Inner Parent to use. By asking two simple questions you can zero in on vague comments thrown at you by your Inner Child and clarify them very quickly. The only catch is that you will have to be familiar with the four categories of needs as they are outlined in the next chapter. Once you have studied the four categories of physical, emotional, mental or social a few times, you will find this method easy to implement.

A side benefit of practicing these steps as the Inner Parent is that your Inner Child will soon learn to become more accurate when telling you what it wants. You will eventually get many more direct statements such as, "I am hungry," or "I want to take an acting class," rather than the indirect or abstract, "Let's cross the street," or "You never do anything for me."

"Thinking Needs"

This process is called "thinking needs" and it works in just about any situation you can imagine. You will have to practice as the Inner Parent, but this is to be expected whenever you learn a new skill. By having a good sense of the four needs categories, you will be able to use this process all the time with your Inner Child.

To achieve the expertise of paying attention and responding appropriately to the needs of your Inner Child, you must have a thorough understanding of needs. Understanding and interpreting the needs of your Inner Child require a new way of thinking. This skill is simple to apply, yet it requires discipline and study on the part of the Inner Parent. To change your Self-Parenting style from negative to positive you must be able to "think needs" very quickly.

Your Inner Child is asking you to meet its needs many times a day. Until you are able to "think needs" as the Inner Parent, your Inner Child will be continually frustrated and you will not know why. Although your Inner Child can be frustrated for many possible reasons, it is always because a need is not being met. "Thinking needs" will enable you to determine which physical, emotional, mental or social need your Inner Child is expressing.

One way of looking at Self-Parenting is to realize that the positive Inner Parent meets the many needs of its Inner Child whereas the negative Inner Parent does not. From another perspective, the positive Inner Child is having its needs met whereas the negative Inner Child is not. Understanding this on a deep level will motivate you to master quickly the skill of thinking needs.

Needs are the key to human happiness. The concept of needs is also the single most important concept underlying the process of communication. The sooner you truly understand the process of communication as the meeting or fulfilling of your needs, the sooner you will be happy and fulfilled.

With all this responsibility it is no wonder the poor Inner Parent is under some pressure. Fortunately, with training and time, any Inner Parent can become skillful at thinking needs. Simply by reading the next chapter, you will become much better at this skill. Once you have internalized this practice of "thinking needs" as an Inner Parent, you will find the technique invaluable.

7

THE NEEDS OF
YOUR INNER CHILD

The Problem

The weak or negative Inner Parent is often unable to differentiate clearly between the numerous types of needs. Without a loving, supporting and nurturing Inner Parent who is trained to recognize the many different needs as they are manifested by the Inner Child, the Inner Child will be continually frustrated and unhappy.

The Solution

The Inner Parent can learn to classify needs into four basic categories — physical, emotional, mental and social. By reading and rereading this chapter, the Inner Parent learns to monitor and interpret the vague statements made by the Inner Child. Whenever the Inner Child is having a problem, the knowledgeable Inner Parent can quickly scan a list of needs to locate the specific one the Inner Child is voicing. Meeting the specific need will create a happy and fulfilled Inner Child.

THE PHYSICAL NEEDS OF YOUR INNER CHILD

Many of the simple, day-to-day interactions of your Self-Parenting style are intimately tied to the meeting of your physical needs. Your Inner Child has physical needs that are essentially the same as those of an outer child. All you must do is apply the knowledge of these classic physical needs to the communication requests of your Inner Child.

The sooner you become aware of your Inner Child's physical needs, the sooner you will be able to provide for them. The sooner you provide for your Inner Child's physical needs, the better both of you will feel. Here are some of the typical physical needs expressed by your Inner Child every day.

The Need for Food

Food is an obvious physical need of your Inner Child; without it you will starve. But how many of you are listening to the messages from your Inner Child about what it wants to eat? Or when? How long does your Inner Child cry out for food before your Inner Parent realizes you are hungry? When you go to a restaurant, how long does it take to pick exactly what you want from the menu? Do you change your mind several times? When your Inner Child is full, do you hear and honor its request to stop eating? Do you give the same care and consideration to the food you prepare for your Inner Child as for your dinner guests?

Your Inner Child will always try to let you know when it is hungry and when it is full. It often has a specific preference for certain food. For example, it may want to eat a certain vegetable. If you give it other vegetables as a substitute, it may or may not accept them. If your Inner Child doesn't accept them, there is no amount or type of other vegetables that will satisfy the Inner Child's need.

The physical requirement for food often turns into an emotional power struggle between the Inner Parent and Inner Child. Initially the Inner Child wants a specific food. For some reason, the Inner Parent doesn't have that food, doesn't want to get that food or doesn't want the Inner Child to eat that food. The next thing you know, the Inner Child and Inner Parent become locked in an Inner Conflict over that decision. Since the issue is never resolved to the satisfaction of the Inner Child, the emotion is carried over to the next eating session.

The physical need for food is more basic than your power squabbles over food. Yet your Inner Child often expresses clear preferences which you, as the Inner Parent, never hear. Frequently what your Inner Child wants to eat is the exact food that will supply missing nutrients or emotional satisfaction, but because you are not paying attention this need goes unmet.

Naturally, just like an outer child, your Inner Child may want food that contains empty calories or harmful additives. In this situation you must make creative use of positive Self-Parenting to create a Win/Win situation for both selves. It is common sense to ensure that the food you eat should be as fresh, healthy and close to its natural state as possible.

Another problem over food occurs when the Inner Parent tells the Inner Child to eat even if it is not hungry. This is like trying to stuff food into an outer child's mouth when he or she is full. Yet the Inner Parent can get away with this behavior because the Inner Child can't make the Inner Parent stop eating.

The Need for Water

The need for water to satisfy thirst is another physical requirement of the Inner Child often missed by the Inner Parent. One day I was talking with a woman who kept licking her lips and swallowing with a dry mouth. I asked her if she was thirsty and she replied, "No, I'm fine." A few minutes later she was repeating her signals of thirst, so I asked her once again if she would like something to drink and again she said no.

Finally, after several more minutes of watching her Inner Child under stress, I went to the kitchen and handed her a glass of water. Her Inner Child grabbed it immediately and drank the whole glass without putting it down. Only after this demonstrative display of thirst did her Inner Parent actually realize that her Inner Child had been thirsty beyond belief and she was simply not aware of it. How many of you do this during the day with your Inner Child?

The Need for Sleep

Sleep is a physiological requirement for the well-being of your body and thus for your Inner Child. Sleeping restfully and dreaming peacefully are among the Inner Child's most profound pleasures. During sleep your Inner Child makes its deepest recovery from the stresses of daily living.

Is your Inner Child tired all the time? Are you listening to your Inner Child when it tells you it feels rested? Do you take powerful drugs such as caffeine or nicotine to whip or stimulate your exhausted Inner Child into action? Are you aware of the physical signs of fatigue your Inner Child gives you? Does your Inner Parent continue to sleep in the morning even though your Inner Child wants to get up and get going?

It takes an aware Inner Parent to interpret the Inner Child's physical needs for sleep and rest. Once you start listening, you will hear many suggestions from your Inner Child on this subject.

The Need for Physical Comfort

Your Inner Child has a need for physical comfort. It often tells you in different ways, "I am physically uncomfortable right now. Please help me." For example, how often are you in a room that is too cold or too hot and even though you are uncomfortable you don't do anything about it? Have you ever worn a sweater or coat in the sun until you almost passed out before you realized you were hot? Have you played a strenuous sport in the heat of the day past the point of sanity? Have you ever sat for a long time with so much pressure on your leg that it became completely numb?

An important aspect of your Inner Parent's role is to monitor the physical comfort of your Inner Child. Are your socks wet, are your feet cold? Is there a draft on your neck? Have you ever gone skiing without gloves or a neck protector because you forgot them at home and you didn't want to pay the inflated prices at the ski lodge? If a friend complained about constant back or neck aches, you might insist he go to a chiropractor; yet when your Inner Child signals the same discomfort, you postpone your visit or don't call for your own appointment.

How about when there is the possibility of rain? Do you bring an umbrella just in case so your Inner Child won't get wet? You would certainly advise others to bring a raincoat so they don't suffer needlessly, but when you look at the sky and your Inner Child says, "Should we go back inside and get our umbrella?" your Inner Parent answers, "No, it's too much hassle."

I know someone who goes surfing even in the dead of winter without a wetsuit. His wife told me that one time some young kids (with winter wetsuits) were on the beach because *they* were too cold to go surfing. Instead, they were amusing themselves by taking bets on how long her husband would live. She said that when he returns from his surf session, he is completely purple and it takes him four to six hours to reverse the hypothermia. Even though his Inner Child loves to surf, he might be taking better care of his physical need to be comfortable by purchasing a wetsuit.

How about the simple act of going to the bathroom? We know that eliminating waste products after eating is a fact of human life. Each Inner Child has its own timing and rhythm for this routine. Yet many times your Inner Child signals its need to go to the bathroom and your Inner Parent is too involved in something else to notice. What if there will be a wait or delay without bathroom facilities? Does the Inner Parent anticipate and think ahead for this eventual need of the Inner Child?

The Need for Order and Protection

Your Inner Child wants to feel safe and protected from physical abuse or danger. This includes feeling secure in your neighborhood, your job environment or your living arrangements. For example, often it is the Inner Child who likes a neat house or apartment. Yet your Inner Parent is too lazy to clean it despite repeated urgings from your Inner Child. Or your Inner Child may want the furniture moved or a plant repositioned in the living room and your Inner Parent never hears the request. Your Inner Child will often give you specific requests concerning your home environment, if you are paying attention.

And what happens if you live in a "bad" neighborhood? Do you take special care to protect your Inner Child and its possessions? You would not leave your doors or windows open or your car unlocked. You would park in a well-lighted area at night. Do you have a neighbor who is constantly bothering your Inner Child with excessive noise? What steps can you take as an Inner Parent to correct the situation?

Another area where the physical needs for order and protection are important to your Inner Child is the work place. Is your environment at work safe? Do you handle dangerous or potentially toxic chemicals? Are you laboring under unsafe working conditions? Is there an air conditioner blowing on your neck all day? Do you talk on the phone for hours with your neck clamping the receiver? Does your boss yell at you and throw your papers on the floor? Your Inner Child will often give you messages concerning its "order and protection" needs during the day when you pay close attention.

The Need to Breathe Fresh Air

Clean air has disappeared in urban environments. There is probably little you can do as an individual about the smog or pollution where you live except move. But are you doing what you can to supply the needs of your Inner Child for fresh air in other ways? For example, have you taken time to go to nature areas with fresh air and do some deep breathing? Are you one of those people who jogs along busy thoroughfares during rush-hour traffic?

Inhaling high levels of carbon monoxide seems the height of abuse or neglect for the physical needs of the Inner Child. Surface streets in your neighborhood are a much saner choice by the Inner Parent.

Do you smoke? Many people say their Inner Child is the one who wants to smoke, but when you examine their Inner Conversations, their Inner Child is willing to stop. Their Inner Parent is the one who doesn't want to quit.

Here is another example of an increasing problem that you might not see as related to your Self-Parenting style. Have you ever entered a restaurant and suddenly realized because of the smell that they must have sprayed DDT that day? Did you eat there anyway, enduring the smell and toxicity? Or did you get up and leave to protect your Inner Child? Have you ever noticed yourself coughing and coughing for weeks and doing nothing as an Inner Parent to determine what is causing the problem?

The Need for Clothing

Your Inner Child has a physical need for clothing to protect and warm itself as well as protect its modesty. This is basic. But did you know that your Inner Child also has strong opinions about the clothes you wear? Since it is the one wearing the clothes, your Inner Child has a big stake in what you put on in the morning. How happy is your Inner Child with your wardrobe? How many days last month did you leave the house without asking your Inner Child if it was satisfied with what you were wearing?

Your Inner Child often tells you its preferences when you shop for clothes. It may or may not want the most practical items, so you may have to try on more clothes than you would like before you can make a decision. You will discover many messages about clothing from your Inner Child when you begin paying attention.

The Need for Exercise

Exercise is also a major physical need. Playing and physical activities are the normal activities of your Inner Child just as they are for an outer child. Your

Inner Child loves the physical exertion and entertainment of exercise, especially if it is performing activities it enjoys.

On the other hand, if you as an Inner Parent are forcing your Inner Child to perform repetitive and boring activities it hates, then you are abusing this need of your Inner Child. If your Inner Child enjoys going to the gym, you won't have any trouble finding the motivation to go. But if your Inner Child hates going to the gym, you might try to find a way to make it more fun.

Perhaps there are reasons why your Inner Child doesn't want to exercise at a certain time or place. Maybe you go to a gym that your Inner Parent thinks is great because it is cheap but your Inner Child hates because it is dirty. Your Inner Child expresses many opinions concerning how it wants its needs met, but you must be paying attention to hear them.

When exercising, your prime concern as the Inner Parent is to find an activity that your Inner Child enjoys and that is beneficial. There are many ways to make exercise fun if your Inner Parent is guiding the exercise in a proper manner.

The Need for Money

Like it or not, your Inner Child has a physical need for money to survive. Without money you are unable to provide many of the other physical needs such as food, shelter and clothing. Therefore, as the Inner Parent, you must work out a way to provide your Inner Child with the money you both need for survival.

Your Inner Child also wants to be employed doing work that it enjoys or at least is neutral toward performing. If your Inner Child hates your job, you will have problems with your Self-Parenting style even when you are not at work. Life is too short to work at a job your Inner Child hates or with people your Inner Child can't stand.

Another aspect of money is that your Inner Child deserves a fair percentage of your income (that it helps to earn) to spend on what it wants. As an Inner

Parent you should determine a percentage or dollar amount of your pay-check to be allocated for your Inner Child to spend as it pleases. This is extra money, beyond what you must spend for normal living expenses. This way it will feel rewarded for the part it plays on the job it works hard to perform. Ten percent seems to be a fair amount for the Inner Child.

The Need for Physical Contact

Your Inner Child also needs the exchange of physical touching with others. This need includes sexual contact, but the exchange of non-sexual physical contact is even more important. Sexual contact alone does not meet your Inner Child's need for physical touch.

On the other hand, your Inner Child may not like to be touched by strangers as a general rule. In this case you should not, as the Inner Parent, force your Inner Child to hug people or be affectionate. You must be ever vigilant to monitor your Inner Child's physical needs in this respect.

These are the basic physical needs. When your Inner Child says that its undefined need is physical, simply run through these choices in your mind so it can choose. Next we will explore some of the typical emotional needs that are associated with the Inner Child.

THE EMOTIONAL NEEDS OF YOUR INNER CHILD

Most people perceive the Inner Child within the context of its emotional needs. They associate the Inner Child with feelings, and of course they are correct. Emotions are the province of the Inner Child. It is the Inner Child who feels emotion, not the Inner Parent. This includes the full range of feelings from happiness to sadness and from love to hate.

There is much more dimensionality to the Inner Child than restricting it to feelings and emotions. From an overall perspective, the physical, mental and social needs of the Inner Child are just as important as its emotional needs. For this chapter, however, the emotional needs of the Inner Child will be emphasized. If your Inner Child says it has an emotional need but you are not sure what it is, choose from this list.

The Need to Feel Enthusiastic

The first and most important need of the Inner Child is to feel intense eagerness or ardent desire — in other words, enthusiasm. Your Inner Child is the natural source of the enthusiasm and energy the Inner Parent must have to pursue an activity. Without enthusiasm, you will constantly have to whip and push your Inner Child into actions which it doesn't really want or care about.

Enthusiasm for life is the natural state of the positive Inner Child. Whenever your Inner Child is resistant or unenthusiastic about an activity, you must seek out the reason. In this situation your Inner Child is often suffering from an important need or concern that is not being considered.

The Need to Be Loved/To Give Love

Your Inner Child has a need to love and be loved. Within the Self-Parenting relationship this is primarily the exchange of attention and caring between the Inner Parent and Inner Child. The Inner Child also enjoys the exchange of love among family and friends as well.

Love and caring emanate from your Inner Child. They are first instilled in the Inner Child by the loving and caring received from your original caretakers. If you did not receive attention and caring as a child, it can be very difficult and time-consuming to give your Inner Child the amount of love and attention it needs. The most effective way to give love to your Inner Child is to do it directly through daily half-hour sessions.

The Need for Attention

Attention is a key desire of every Inner Child. Receiving attention on a regular basis from the Inner Parent is the proof the Inner Child needs to feel loved and lovable. Every Inner Child wants to believe that its Inner Parent truly loves and cares about it. This need is fulfilled by the Inner Parent scheduling daily half-hour sessions with the Inner Child. No matter what else may happen, if you practice daily sessions faithfully, your Inner Child will feel secure about receiving the love and attention it needs from the Inner Parent.

Most people are not aware that they have an Inner Child. Because their Inner Child is unknown to them, it feels completely ignored. In this circumstance the Inner Child has no possibility of feeling loved, accepted or praised by its Inner Parent. This state is very unproductive and leaves both Inner Selves feeling unfulfilled.

The Need to Be Happy

Your Inner Child has a need to be happy. Happiness comes from feeling loved and enjoying daily activities. This need is satisfied when the internal potential that the Inner Child feels is realized. If this need is not met, the

Inner Child will always feel incomplete or that something is missing in its life. If this need is met, even though external circumstances may be extremely trying, the internal happiness of the Inner Child will be assured.

The Need to Have Fun

The Inner Child enjoys a natural need to play, have fun or to be entertained. Even in poverty-stricken areas such as the slums of Rio or the backwaters of The Amazon, young children spend their time playing and inventing games using whatever materials they have on hand. You may not live under such dire circumstances, but if your Inner Child is not allowed to have its need for fun met, you will experience a lack of fulfillment.

The Need for a Positive Home Life

Your Inner Child has an emotional need for a positive home life, not only within the confines of your Inner Conversations but also within the physical surroundings of your home. The safety and comfort of a positive home environment are very important to your Inner Child. It wants to have fun when appropriate and to enjoy peace and quiet when appropriate. It enjoys being surrounded by possessions it loves, such as pictures, furniture and colorful decorations.

Part of this need also includes living with pleasant people. A roommate situation that constantly has your Inner Child on edge is an example of not meeting its needs for a positive home life. No matter what else happens in life, if you know that you can go home to relax and recharge, you are meeting this need.

The Need to Express Opinions

Your Inner Child has a need and a right to express its opinions. Its opinions should be heard and considered by the Inner Parent even if they are crazy or off the mark. Often the Inner Child just wants to make a point or an observation about a situation, but when this opinion is missed or ignored by the Inner Parent, the Inner Child feels slighted or depressed. This is the same need that most of us feel when we are involved in outer relationships with our family, friends or work associates. Even if our opinion doesn't influence the main decision, we still want to be heard and acknowledged.

The Need for Creative Expression

Your Inner Child has a need to express itself creatively. This need can be met in a great variety of ways including hobbies, the fine arts, community involvement, etc. These activities translate the internal feelings of the Inner Child into emotional expression. The source of your creativity comes from the intuitive and emotional range of your Inner Child's feelings and motivation.

The Need for Privacy/Alone Time

Your Inner Child needs specific time in which to have the full attention of the Inner Parent. This time can have different purposes, but the fact that it is just the Inner Child alone with the full attention of the Inner Parent is what counts. This is the need that most people associate with being alone and "recharging oneself."

Preferably this is active time in which the Inner Child can air its grievances, state its opinions or viewpoints and have its side of a situation heard. This time could also be spent in meditative, contemplative or interactive activities with the Inner Parent. In these modern times, very few people spend solitary time between just their Inner Parent and Inner Child. Fulfilling this need is perhaps the most important value of the SELF-PARENTING Program.

As your Inner Parent becomes more aware of your Inner Child's emotional needs in daily life, you will find it easier and easier to meet these needs directly. Fulfilling your Inner Child's emotional needs is the most obvious way to achieve the happiness and contentment that most of us seek.

THE MENTAL NEEDS OF YOUR INNER CHILD

Your Inner Child has a unique kind of genius which is expressed through its mental needs. Your Inner Child loves mental exploration which is often motivated by unfulfilled feelings or desires. In fact, many successful scientists and inventors such as Albert Einstein and Thomas Edison have described their experiences of getting in touch with their intuitive sides (the Inner Child) in order to solve problems or create inventions. Since the Inner Child is the intuitive side of you, it makes sense that your Inner Child has intellectual needs and desires.

Another aspect of mental needs concerns your Inner Child's desires and fantasies. These have a mental quality to them as they are stimulated through interaction with other people, exposure to the media or life experiences. When considering the mental needs, remember that your Inner Child is a completely separate personality with its own distinct viewpoints. Even though it is right-brain oriented, it has a thinking aspect to go along with its emotional/feeling side. Your Inner Child can be very opinionated. The more you understand the mental side of the Inner Child, the more interesting you will find it. Your Inner Child has a number of mental needs.

The Need to Explore

The need to explore new ideas and concepts is a mental need of your Inner Child. The positive Inner Child naturally views life as fun, challenging and intriguing. It loves to experience a new adventure or to explore areas of life that it hasn't been exposed to yet. It wants to ask questions, figure things out, or discover how something works. This curiosity is easily seen in the outer child who is filled with questions and wonder about nature. When you are exposed to new subject areas or exotic travels, it is often the Inner Child who is intrigued by the new experience.

From the Inner Child's perspective, this mental need is more associated with the general aspects of a situation than with specific technical material. The Inner Parent must also be involved to provide the willingness for long-term study or deeper scientific understanding. What most people don't realize is that the mental interest and/or support of the Inner Child is a significant contribution to sustained studies even in technical areas.

Your Inner Child was born with an exploring, searching and testing spirit. Your Inner Child's curiosity and absorption must be guided to worthwhile activities by your Inner Parent. A meaningful life comes from matching the internal curiosity and natural talents of your Inner Child with the external goals and leadership of your Inner Parent. This creates the mutual involvement for enjoying life which is the foundation of happiness for both Inner Selves. The positive stimulation and encouragement of your Inner Child's interests are at the core of positive Self-Parenting.

The Need to Be Taught

The Inner Child has a tremendous built-in desire to succeed. In order for this need to be fulfilled, the Inner Child must be taught. This point is often not realized by the Inner Parent. An explanation or teaching discussion is often an important need of your Inner Child before beginning a new experience such as taking a class, buying a computer or moving your office. Explanations that include what you will see, what you are doing and why you are doing it are very helpful to the Inner Child when beginning new activities.

Your Inner Child is often ambitious. It's the role of the Inner Parent to nurture this ambition with logistical support and guidance based on "real world" concerns. If properly nurtured, your Inner Child will continue to grow and learn throughout your lifetime. Its interest and enthusiasm will always be alert and present. At age 60 your Inner Child may be trying to figure out new math, or it may take up a new skill such as computer programming, something that didn't even exist when it was a child.

The Need to Learn

As a child you loved to learn. The more you learned, the better you felt. You were fascinated by explanations of how things worked and you took in information like a sponge. Outer children love to converse and ask questions. They are very aware and observant. Because of their constant need to know, they often ask questions that are difficult to answer.

In the same way your Inner Child has a natural sense of identity, and that identity has an agenda of subjects it wants to explore or learn about. As an Inner Parent you must pay attention to your Inner Child's needs in this area. Providing an environment of stimulating learning opportunities will keep your relationship exciting and provocative.

The Need for Encouragement

The Inner Child has a need to be helped and encouraged when exploring its interests or talents. Whether beginning a new project or experiencing frustration with a long-term project, your Inner Parent must provide encouragement and motivation for the Inner Child. The positive Inner Parent will develop ways to encourage and allow the Inner Child to be creative, playful and use its imagination.

If your Inner Child has a strong desire to achieve something, you must be willing to support its pursuits. The Inner Parent can find many opportunities to encourage the Inner Child to be inventive or to be ambitious. If this subject area is outside the mainstream activities of your life, you must help your Inner Child to pursue its interests.

The Inner Child also learns through mimicking those around it. Therefore, you can help your Inner Child derive encouragement and motivation simply by being with people doing the activities it wants to learn. Meet this need by providing situations supportive to the learning of the Inner Child. If the Inner Child can be surrounded by people actually practicing what it wants to learn, it will absorb information at a much faster rate.

The Need to Be Recognized

Your Inner Child has a need to be recognized for its unique personality, work or achievement. This is more of a mental or artistic need than the purely emotional need for expression described under emotional needs. For example, your Inner Child may enjoy playing music as a means of self-expression, but it may also have a desire to enter and win some music competitions. This need is fulfilled through sustained acts of creativity which win the approval of others or through learning or mastering new skills.

The negative Inner Parent can often get in the way of this need of the Inner Child. The Inner Parent may be afraid to enter a contest because it is afraid it will lose. Or the Inner Parent may not want to pay the $20 fee required. If the Inner Parent is weak or lazy, the Inner Child's desire for artistic expression will go to waste, creating a difficult and negative condition within your Inner Conversations.

The self-confidence enjoyed by your Inner Child is the result of the way your Inner Parent treats the learning desires of your Inner Child. When you demonstrate acceptance and praise for your Inner Child's mental needs, it will feel self-confident naturally. If your Inner Child does not feel self-confident, this means that you, as the Inner Parent, are doing an inadequate job of supporting your Inner Child's mental needs. Remember, an Inner Child involved with a project of interest is a happy Inner Child.

The Need to Communicate

Your Inner Child is always expanding mentally. It is full of determination to discover its limits. As it is formulating its personality, it must communicate its knowledge and perspective with others. Much of this takes place within your Inner Conversations, but it also wants to communicate with others. It wants to test what it learns and see what effect this knowledge has on others. Your Inner Child often has new ideas or observations that it wants to add to group conversations. Engaging in half-hour sessions gives your Inner Child a daily opportunity to express itself with you, the Inner Parent. The positive Inner Parent also provides ample opportunities for the Inner Child to meet its need to communicate with others as well.

Simply put, developing a positive Self-Parenting style is the easiest way to meet your physical, emotional and mental needs. For many people, the mental need of their Inner Child is the neglected area preventing their happiness within their Inner Conversations.

THE SOCIAL NEEDS OF BOTH INNER SELVES

Your Inner Child's physical, emotional and mental needs are (or are not) provided for by your Inner Parent. Your social needs, on the other hand, are provided for through your relationships with others. Technically speaking, your Inner Conversations are where you would meet your Inner Child's physical, emotional and mental needs. As such, you, the Inner Parent, are ultimately responsible for providing these needs to your Inner Child within your Inner Conversations.

On the other hand, you and your Inner Child act as a team in your outer relationships. Socially speaking, the Inner Selves have needs together which only outer relationships with others can fulfill. For example, you cannot meet the social needs provided by a husband/wife relationship from within your Inner Conversations. Your spouse will have to meet these relationship needs for you. In the same way, if you are unhappy with your boss/employee relationship, you will have to work that out with the specific person.

What can happen in outer relationships, however, is that the two Inner Selves often have completely different concerns and motivations as to meeting social needs. You must be an astute Inner Parent to pay attention and respond appropriately to your Inner Child's needs in a social relationship if they differ from the needs of the Inner Parent. With this in mind, here are some Self-Parenting guidelines for the Inner Parent concerning the outer family, social and work relationships.

Your participation in outer relationships should be divided according to the natural strengths of the two selves. Ideally, your outer relationships combine the Inner Child's enthusiasm with the Inner Parent's rational decision-making. To benefit socially, both selves must feel fulfilled within their respective roles and allow their energies to flow naturally when interacting with others in a relationship.

Your Inner Parent and Inner Child have specific needs in each outer relationship which you must be aware of as an Inner Parent. It is your job as the Inner Parent to evaluate the positive or negative effects that outer relationships have on the quality of your Inner Conversations. You will need to evaluate how your outer relationships affect your Inner Conversations on a daily basis.

For example, your Inner Child may feel a desperate need for a boyfriend/girlfriend relationship at any cost. Because of this need, your Inner Child may be willing to put up with an extremely negative partner just to be in a relationship. In this situation, the Inner Parent must consider the Inner Child's needs, but not allow it to make decisions or take actions that will have known negative consequences. If the Inner Parent lets the Inner Child fulfill its social need with a negative person, the benefits of the relationship will ultimately be outweighed by the emotional costs.

With this in mind, let's look at the social needs of both Inner Selves within the Self-Parenting relationship.

The Need To Learn And Follow Sensible Social Rules

Both Inner Selves have a need to learn and follow sensible social rules. This includes not only following the proper protocol in social and business situations, but also having respect for other people's needs, opinions and differences. Many social rules are determined by the social circumstances of your relationships. Respecting these rules is essential if you are to earn and keep the respect of your peers. If you choose to ignore these rules, there may be dramatic effects on your well-being as reflected within your Inner Conversations.

The Need To Learn And Practice Positive Social Skills

Both Inner Selves need to develop positive and basic social skills such as practicing good manners, sharing with and listening to others, setting a positive example and protecting your needs in a relationship. Part of your role as an Inner Parent involves teaching social responsibility skills to your Inner Child. For example, perhaps your Inner Child is afraid to make speeches or phone calls that are part of the duties of a new job. In this case you must teach (or get someone else to teach) your Inner Child how to accomplish these basic tasks. Perhaps you would join a speaking club or arrange to take a series of weekend trainings on sales procedures.

The Need To Study And Learn Communication Skills

A major part of learning to interact with others in relationships is developing positive communication skills. You are learning much about positive communication skills through skillful interaction with your Inner Child during half-hour sessions. Outer relationships require many additional skills which must become a natural part of your personality. In this situation you might read recommended books on communication and put the ideas and principles into practice.

The Need To Resolve Relationship Conflicts

One of the most important areas of successful human relationships is learning how to resolve conflicts with others. You can use the same eight steps of Inner Conflict resolution you learned in Self-Parenting to resolve conflicts in your outer relationships as well. This will involve practicing the steps you use with your Inner Child with the person with whom you are having the conflict. Fortunately, every step can be enacted in exactly the same manner. In fact, the techniques to resolve Inner Conflicts were developed from methods used to resolve outer conflicts.

The Need To Promote Social Functioning In The "Real World"

You and your Inner Child must make decisions jointly when deciding what you want to be, do or have in life. As the Inner Parent, you are directly responsible for following through with any decisions made by the two Inner Selves. This includes how you spend your free time, whom to spend it with and what you want to do together.

By now you realize this planning must include input from both Inner Selves or your goals and projects will be unsuccessful. For example, career planning involves both your Inner Parent and Inner Child. These decisions are intimately tied to how well you meet your needs in your work relationships. Another recommendation is to make sure as an Inner Parent that both you and your Inner Child are completely happy before choosing a marriage partner. Every social relationship has particular circumstances that may reflect opposing needs between the Inner Selves.

The Need To Be Recognized And Feel Part of a Group

The Inner Child enjoys the social interaction that comes from being in contact with other Inner Children. It has fun when it is able to join or take part in a group of people with similar interests. Part of this need is peer acceptance and may involve taking a role as a leader or follower in a group.

This need to be part of a group is important to the Inner Child in all three areas of human relationships: family, social and work. The Inner Child enjoys helping, being a part of things and pleasing others. When you feel conflicts over your social obligations, your Inner Child often wants to do the socially acceptable thing; your Inner Parent may be the one who doesn't. Unless you are listening carefully, you will not know for sure.

The Inner Child, being the non-verbal and intuitive self, is often more sensitive to the proper protocol in social situations. Many times it automatically knows the constructive actions to take or sensible rules to follow with others. If it doesn't, its natural innocence is usually enough to earn the friendship of others who will teach you the proper guidelines to follow.

However, if your Inner Child is lacking in good manners or the social skills of sharing, listening and respecting the opinions of others, your Inner Parent must teach the Inner Child these important skills. Your Inner Child must be taught positive values including the concepts of honesty, responsibility and commitment to your relationships. If you did not have a positive role model for this when you were young, then you must use your half-hour sessions for this purpose now.

A large part of your Inner Parent's social role within your Self-Parenting style is to evaluate the positive or negative effects of your social behaviors. Many of the permutations and vagaries of modern social interaction can contribute to Inner Conflicts between the values of the Inner Parent and Inner Child. These issues must be sorted out and resolved within your half-hour sessions. You will need the help of both Inner Selves to practice the conflict resolution skills you use in your Inner Conversations in your outer relationships as well.

Here is one example of the infinite possibilities. A woman was having a conflict with her ex-husband as to whether or not to attend a family gathering. All her children and grandchildren were going to be there and part of her wanted to go. However, her ex-husband's new girlfriend said she would feel uncomfortable, so she had asked the husband that his ex-wife not come. The woman's Inner Child was extremely upset and insisted that it be there at the family gathering to assert its presence.

On the other hand, her Inner Parent didn't want to go so as not to make waves. Nor did she want the negative situation involving her ex-husband to flare up. Both Inner Selves had social needs in this situation, although they were in complete opposition. The divorcee needed to perform an Inner Conflict resolution to determine which course to take.

Knowledge and understanding of the basic principles of Self-Parenting are the ultimate key to conducting your outer relationships. If you know how the relationship between you and your Inner Child works, you will find it much easier to understand how your outer relationships work. The true success or failure of your outer relationships is ultimately based on the proportion of positive to negative traits in your Self-Parenting style.

NEW BEGINNING

The purpose of this book is to give you, a practitioner of the Self-Parenting Program, a greater understanding of your role and responsibilities as an Inner Parent. My goal was to bring you to the threshold of an unprecedented awareness of the dynamics involved in the relationship of your Inner Parent and Inner Child. By integrating the knowledge of your Inner Child's needs into your Self-Parenting style, you can achieve a condition of confidence and knowledge that heretofore has been inaccessible.

Although this knowledge has been presented in a manner as simple and easy to understand as possible, I caution you not underestimate the value of what you have been given as an Inner Parent. These guidelines for understanding and accessing the needs of your Inner Child have been hard won.

You will discover many layers of "quantum depth" to the information in this book. Many months, possibly even years, of dedicated half-hour sessions may be required before you can internalize these principles fully into your daily life. When this does happen, both you and your Inner Child will enjoy a relationship of commitment, trust and joy that few people have ever achieved.

A Gift for You
$15

To be applied toward tuition for any
SELF-PARENTING® Program Seminar.

Signature _____

YES! Please contact me with information about:

❑ The SELF-PARENTING® Program Seminar
❑ Quantity discounts on **SELF-PARENTING** books
❑ Having John Pollard speak at my convention or meeting
❑ Starting a SELF-PARENTING® Support Group in my area
❑ Self-Parenting modules on specific subjects
❑ Self-Parenting Professional Course materials (therapists only)
❑ Telephone consultations
❑ Therapist referral in my area   **SPP-1**

Name: _____
Address: _____
City: _____ State: _____ Zip: _____
Home Phone (_____) _____
Work Phone (_____) _____

**Please enclose a stamped, self-addressed, #10
envelope for rapid reply.**

Acceptable as payment along with
deposit as registration for any
SELF-PARENTING® Program Seminar.
To redeem this gift certificate call

310-457-1140
or toll free
1-800-458-0091

You may also detach and mail
the information postcard below.

Mail To:

The SELF-PARENTING® Program
P. O. Box 6535
Malibu, CA 90265